a guide to growing
glorious climbers

a guide to growing
glorious climbers

Richard Bird

LORENZ BOOKS

This edition first published by Lorenz Books

© Anness Publishing Limited, 2000

Lorenz Books is an imprint of Anness Publishing Limited
Hermes House, 88–89 Blackfriars Road, London SE1 8HA

Published in the USA by Lorenz Books
Anness Publishing Inc
27 West 20th Street, New York, NY 10011; (800) 354-9657

This edition distributed in Canada by Raincoast Books
8680 Cambie Street, Vancouver, British Columbia V6P 6M9

ISBN 0-7548-0550-6

A CIP catalogue record is available from the British Library

Publisher: Joanna Lorenz
Project Editor: Alison Macfarlane
Editor: Deborah Savage
Designer: Caroline Reeves
Photographer: Jonathan Buckley

Jacket
Design and Art Direction: Clare Reynolds
Front cover image: Flowers & Foliage Picture Library/Gill Orsman

Previously published as *Step-by-Step Glorious Climbers*

CONTENTS

INTRODUCTION

To anyone creating a garden, climbing plants are an essential ingredient. Not only do they provide both flower and foliage effects, as do most other plants, but they give vertical emphasis to a garden. Climbers carry their colour up and away from the ground, creating a three-dimensional effect. Trees and shrubs also do this, but they are much more limited, as their shape is predetermined. Climbers, however, can be used to create slim pillars of colour, or wide sheets of it.

Climbers can be used in many different ways. They can decorate buildings by covering the walls, transforming their appearance. This is particularly useful if the building has an ugly appearance, such as a concrete garage, or if its lines need to be softened. Walls covered in plants in this way also provide a good backdrop for the rest of the garden.

If they are grown on trellises or fences, climbers can be used as boundaries, to provide privacy and, again, to make a backdrop for other plants. An ugly wire fence is much enhanced by being covered with a clematis, for example. Similarly, trellises can be used as internal dividers, separating different parts of the garden from each other. Climbers over trellises provide a screen but, at the same time, unlike a solid screen, allow tempting glimpses of what lies beyond.

Formal arches through these screens can be covered in climbers, as can arches set in other parts of the garden, purely as a decorative effect along paths. Arches can be combined to form a pergola or walkway. These can be superb features in a garden, especially when they are dripping with the flowers of wisteria or rose.

Right: Rosa 'Cupid' trained on a rope.

Adding a back to an arch gives you an arbour, a shady place in which to sit. Arbours can be small and discreet, suitable for intimate trysts, or larger, with plenty of room for a table for alfresco meals. They are particularly delightful places in the evening, especially if you choose scented climbers to grow over them.

Climbers can also be used somewhat in the fashion of trees and shrubs, if you allow them to climb up tripods or pillars, to make columns of varying sizes of flowering and foliage plants. These can be permanent fixtures in the garden or they can be temporary, so that the design can be changed from time to time. A more versatile form of temporary display can be created by using temporary supports such as pea-sticks, up which annuals – sweet peas, for example – can scramble.

The gardener is not restricted to growing a single climber up a support but can grow two or even three different plants together. With the right choice of plants this allows for a sequence of flowering throughout the season. A similar effect can be achieved by allowing climbing plants to scramble up through trees and shrubs. Climbers offer a very wide range of flower colour and foliage effects. As with trees and shrubs, there are climbers that will provide a vivid splash of autumn colour as well as those that produce colourful berries or other fruit. There are also fragrantly flowering climbers, which are best planted near open windows or in places where the gardener sits and relaxes.

The possibilities for using and combining climbers are almost endless; this book will help to stimulate the imagination as well as provide answers to many practical problems, so that the gardener can create a truly wonderful garden by making the most of climbing plants.

Above: Rosa *'Bobby James' scrambles over a trellis archway.*

Below: Clematis *'Nelly Moser' trained by the front door of a house provides a warm welcome to visitors.*

Right: *A mixture of climbers clamber over a summerhouse and arbour to create a shady sitting place.*

Preparing the Soil for Planting

The key to any successful gardening is good soil preparation. This is particularly true in the case of climbers, because the plants are likely to stay in the same position for many years. Inadequate attention to preparation at the outset is difficult to remedy once the plant has put down its roots and become established.

THE IMPORTANCE OF PREPARATION

It is extremely important to clear the soil of perennial weeds. If only one piece of many of these remains, it will soon regrow and be impossible to eradicate, as the roots become entwined in those of the climber. Once the planting area is completely cleared, however, it is not such a difficult task to remove seedlings and keep the bed and the plants clear from then on.

Digging is important as it breaks up the soil, allowing moisture and air to enter, both being vital to the well-being of the plant. The process also allows the gardener to keep an eye out for any soil pests. Dig the soil some time before you intend to plant the bed; digging in autumn and planting in early spring, after checking for any emerging weeds, is ideal.

As you dig the soil, incorporate well-rotted organic material. This is very important; not only does it provide food for the plants but it also helps to improve the structure of the soil. The fibrous material helps to break down the soil to a crumbly consistency, which allows free drainage of excess water and, at the same time, acts as a reservoir to hold sufficient water for the plants without water-logging them.

The final breaking down of the soil with a rake is more for aesthetic appeal than usefulness; the planting area will look more attractive if it has a smooth tilth than if it is left rough.

If possible, prepare an area of at least 1–1.2 m (3–4 ft) in diameter, so that the roots can spread out into good soil as they grow.

SOIL CONDITIONERS

Chipped or composted bark – little nutritional value, but a good mulch.
Farmyard manure – rich in nutrients but often contains weed seed. Good conditioner.
Garden compost – good nutrient value and very good as a conditioner.
Leaf mould – composted leaves. Good nutritional value. Excellent conditioner and mulch.
Peat – not very suitable as it breaks down too quickly and has little nutritional value.

1 Using a chemical spray is the only way to be sure of completely eradicating perennial weeds. Use a non-persistent herbicide, which breaks down when it comes into contact with the soil. It is vital always to follow the instructions on the pack exactly, not only for the obvious safety reasons but also to ensure you use the correct dose to kill all the weeds in the area first time.

2 If the turf to be removed does not include perennial weeds, or the soil is friable enough for the weed's roots to be removed by hand, it is safer to remove the turf by slicing it off with a spade. Stack the turves in a heap, grass-side down, and use them as compost (soil mix) when they have broken down.

3 Dig over the soil and, as you dig, remove any weed roots and large stones. Double dig, if the subsoil needs to be broken up. Add as much well-rotted organic material as you can to the soil before it is planted, in order to improve its condition.

4 Add the compost (soil mix) or manure to the soil as you dig, or spread it over the top after all weed roots have been removed, and fork it in.

5 If you dig in the autumn, leave the soil for the winter weather to break down; at any other time, break the soil down by hand into a reasonably fine tilth. Use a rake or hoe to break down the larger lumps of soil, until the bed has an even appearance.

Right: *Ivy can be trained around shapes to create topiary. The ivy should be regularly clipped to keep it compact and to retain its shape. The smaller-leaved* Hedera helix *is the best form to use.*

Planting Climbers

There are so many different types of climbers that you are bound to be able to choose one that is suitable for any place in the garden. As always, though, the trick is to match up the plant and the planting position correctly.

CHOOSING A POSITION

Probably the most important thing to remember about planting a climber is that it is essential to pause and consider whether you are planting it in the right place. Once planted, with the roots spreading and the stems attached to their supports, it is very difficult to move a climber successfully. Once it has grown to its full size, if you realise that you have got the site wrong, you will have a choice of living with your mistake or scrapping the plant and starting all over again with another one. So, think carefully about the position of any climber you plan to introduce.

As well as considering how the climber looks in its intended position, there is a practical consideration. If you are planting against a wall or fence, the plant should be set a distance away, as the ground immediately adjacent to such structures is usually very dry. Similarly, if a pole or post has been concreted in or simply surrounded with rammed earth, it is best for the roots of your climber to be planted a short distance out and the stems led to the support with canes or sticks.

Most plants should be planted at the same depth as they were in their pot or in the nursery bed (usually indicated by the soil line on the stem). The main exception is clematis, which should be planted 5 cm (2 in)

deeper, so that the base of the stems is covered.

Mulching around the climber helps to preserve moisture and to keep the weeds down. A variety of methods can be used for mulching; any of them will be of benefit at this stage in helping the climber to establish itself quickly.

PLANTING TIMES

Traditionally, climbers were planted, when the weather allowed, between mid-autumn and mid-spring, but most climbers are now sold as container-grown plants and these can be planted at any time of the year, as long as the weather is not too extreme. Bare-rooted climbers have the best chance of survival if planted at the traditional time. Avoid planting any climber when the weather is very hot and dry, or when there are drying winds. In winter, avoid times when the ground is waterlogged or frozen.

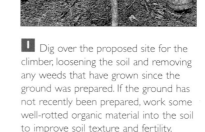

1 Dig over the proposed site for the climber, loosening the soil and removing any weeds that have grown since the ground was prepared. If the ground has not recently been prepared, work some well-rotted organic material into the soil to improve soil texture and fertility.

2 Before planting, add a general or specialist shrub fertilizer to the soil at the dosage recommended on the packet. Work the fertilizer into the soil around the planting area with a fork. A slow-release organic fertilizer, such as bonemeal, is best.

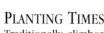

3 Water the plant in the pot. Dig a hole that is much wider than the rootball of the plant. Place the soil evenly around the hole, so that it can easily be worked in around the plant. The hole should be away from any compacted soil, near a support and at least 30 cm (12 in) away from a wall or fence. Before removing the plant from its pot, stand it in the hole, to make certain that the depth and width are correct.

4 Place a cane or stick across the hole; the top of the rootball should be at the same level. Dig deeper or add soil to the bottom of the hole, as necessary, to bring it up to the correct height. Remove the plant from the pot, being careful that none of the soil falls away from the rootball. If the plant is in a polythene (plastic) container rather than a pot, cut the bag away rather than pulling it off. Holding the plant steady, pull in the soil from around the hole, filling in around the rootball. Firm as you go, with your hands, and then finally firm down all around the plant with your foot, making certain that there are no cavities or large air pockets.

5 Train the stems of the climber up individual canes to their main support. Tie the stems in with string or plastic ties. Even twining plants or plants with tendrils will need this initial help. Spread them out, so that they ultimately cover the whole of their support. Water the plant in well.

6 Put a layer of mulch around the plant, to help preserve the moisture and prevent weed growth.

Right: *The delicate bells of* Clematis viticella *hang suspended in mid-air.*

Providing Support for Climbers 1

When considering the choice and position of a climbing plant, it is important to take into account the method by which it climbs. While an ivy will support itself with modified roots on a brick wall, a rose, which is used to scrambling through bushes in the wild, will need to be tied to wires or trellis that has been attached to the wall.

CLIMBING HABITS

When buying a climbing plant, always consider the way it climbs and check that it is suitable for your purpose. If you want to cover a wall, and money is tight, an ivy is the best choice as it will cost no more than the plant, whereas the rose will also incur the price of the supporting structure. On the other hand, if you later want to paint the wall, it will be impossible to remove the ivy to do so, while a rose on a hinged or clipped trellis can be moved away from the wall to allow the operation to go ahead.

CLINGING CLIMBERS

True climbers are able to attach themselves to their supports. To do this, they have roots or modified roots that grip firmly on the surface of the support. They will attach themselves to any surface, including smooth ones such as glass and plastic. They need little attention, except for cutting them back from around windows and periodically cutting them off at the top of the wall so that they do not foul gutters or creep under tiles. If a wall is in good condition, there is little to fear from these climbers in terms of damage that they might inflict.

Above: Hydrangea anomala petiolaris *clings to wall surfaces by putting out modified roots.*

Right: *Clinging plants will cover any vertical surface without needing any support.*

CLINGING CLIMBERS
Hedera canariensis (Canary Island ivy)
Hedera colchica (Persian ivy)
Hedera helix (common ivy)
Hydrangea anomala petiolaris (climbing hydrangea)
Parthenocissus henryana (Chinese Virginia creeper)
Parthenocissus quinquefolia (Virginia creeper)
Parthenocissus tricuspida (Boston ivy)

CLIMBERS THAT USE TENDRILS

Many climbing plants have adapted themselves so that, although they do not cling to a smooth support, they can attach themselves to branches and other protrusions by means of tendrils. These are modified stems, or even leaves, which curl round the support.

Tendril plants will not climb up a wall unless there is already another plant on it or unless there is a mesh that they can attach themselves to. If a trellis or wires are used and the supporting strands are far apart, the stems will wave about until they are long enough to find something to which to cling; you may need to tie them in, to prevent them from breaking off. Closely woven mesh or another well-branched plant or tree provide the best supports for this type of climber.

CLIMBERS THAT USE TENDRILS

Campsis radicans
    (trumpet creeper)
Clematis
Cobaea scandens
    (cathedral bells)
Lathyrus (peas)
Mutisia
Vitis (vine)

Right: *The overall effect of a wall covered entirely by clematis is a mass of flower and foliage.*

Below: *Clematis puts out tendrils that entwine round a supporting structure, such as wire netting or another plant.*

Providing Support for Climbers 2

SCRAMBLING CLIMBERS

In the wild, apart from those that cling to cliffs, most climbers are supported by other plants. While some have adapted themselves to twine or use tendrils, the majority just push themselves up through the supporting plant, using its framework of branches and twigs as their support. Use this technique in the garden by allowing climbers to ramble up through shrubs and trees.

However, if the climbers are needed for a more formal situation, such as over a pergola or up a trellis or wall, artificial supports will be required. As the plants have no natural way of attaching themselves to wires or trellis, the gardener will have to tie them in with string or plant ties. This should be done at regular intervals, to ensure that the plant is well supported along its whole length.

1 Use special lead-headed nails to attach the stems of scramblers to walls.

2 The malleable lead head can be wrapped around the stem to secure it.

TYPES OF TIES

There are various different materials for tying in stems. String is the most readily available and the cheapest. Use soft garden string for short-term (up to a year) tying in and tarred string for longer periods. Special twists made from thin wire covered with plastic "wings" are sold for garden use, although the version provided with plastic food bags is just as good.

Above: *Materials for tying in climbers* (left to right): *heavy-duty plastic tie; plastic twist tie; narrow plastic tie; tarred string; soft garden string.*

These are best used as temporary ties. Of more permanent use are plastic ties, which come in various sizes, from those suitable for holding stems, to those that will cope with small tree-trunks.

Right: *Take advantage of scrambling climbers' natural habit of growing through other plants by growing a rose through an old apple tree.*

SCRAMBLING CLIMBERS

Akebia
Actinidia (some)
Bougainvillea
Eccremocarpus scaber (Chilean glory flower)
Fallopia baldschuanica (Russian vine)
Passiflora (passion-flower)
Plumbago capensis

Rhodochiton atrosanguineus
Rosa (rose)
Solanum (nightshade)
Thunbergia alata (black-eyed Susan)
Trachelospermum
Tropaeolum (nasturtium)
Vinca (periwinkle)

TWINING PLANTS

Some climbers twine their stems round the support as they grow. Plants that adopt this technique can be grown up poles or trellis, or through trees and shrubs. The stems automatically twist round their support, so little attention is required except to tie in any wayward shoots that might thrash around in the wind and get damaged.

Right: *The stems of twining climbers wind themselves round any support they can find as they grow, so, once you have provided the support, they will do the rest.*

Below: *Here, a hop has covered a metal arch with a shower of green leaves, supported by a mass of curling stems.*

TWINING CLIMBERS
Actinidia (some)
Humulus lupulus (hop)
Ipomoea (morning glory)
Lonicera (honeysuckle)
Phaseolus (climbing beans)

WALL SHRUBS

In gardening parlance, the term "climbing plants" is often liberally interpreted to include any plants that are grown up against walls. This can, in fact, include more or less any shrub. Generally, however, there are some shrubs that are best suited to this position, either because of their appearance or because they need the protection of the wall against the vagaries of the weather. Some are strong enough shrubs not to need support, except, perhaps, to be tied the wall to prevent them from being blown forward. Others need a more rigid support and should be tied into wires or a framework to keep them steady.

Above: Pyracantha *is a perfect wall shrub; it has flowers in the early summer and colourful berries in the autumn. Its branches are viciously thorned, making it a good burglar deterrent to plant on walls around windows.*

WALL SHRUBS
Abutilon
Azara
Carpenteria californica
Ceanothus (Californian lilac)
Cotoneaster
Euonymus fortunei
Magnolia
Pyracantha (firethorn)
Teucrium fruticans
   (shrubby germander)

Weeding and Mulching

For both the health and appearance of a climber, it is essential that it is kept weed-free. Rank grass growing up through a rose, for example, destroys the appearance of the plant and is awkward to remove without getting scratched by the thorns.

WEEDING

Once the pervasive roots of perennial weeds become established amongst the roots of the climber, they are very difficult to remove, so it is essential to prevent them from establishing themselves, or to remove them as soon as they appear. The first requisite of healthy climbers is to prepare the soil thoroughly before planting. Every piece of perennial weed should be either removed by hand or killed off with a herbicide.

Once the climber is planted, weed around it regularly with a trowel or hand hoe. Any perennials that arise from small pieces of root left in the soil should be dug out, as should any suckers, and any seedlings should be hoed off.

It is inevitable that there will be some annual weeds appearing from time to time around your climber, but, if these are removed before they set their seed, their numbers will gradually drop as the reserve of seed in the soil is used up.

MULCHING

Once the soil is clean, applying a mulch will do a great deal to help. It will not prevent perennial weeds that are already established from coming up but it will prevent seed in the soil from germinating. A wide variety of materials can be used. Organic ones are best because, as well as forming a mulch, they slowly decompose into the soil, adding to its structure and fertility, benefiting the plant in the longer term as well.

1 A border with open soil without any kind of mulch is prone to weeds and to the loss of moisture.

2 Grass cuttings are readily available in most gardens. They are not the most attractive form of mulch but can be used effectively at the back of borders, where they are not easily seen. Do not heap them on thicker than 5 cm (2 in) or they may heat up too much as they decompose, harming the plant. Do not use cuttings from lawns that have recently been treated with a lawn herbicide which might harm the plant.

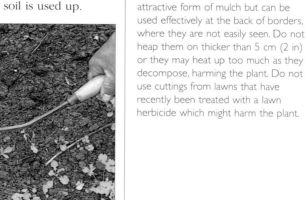

1 The advantage of hand-weeding is that you can thoroughly check what weeds are present and can take more rigorous action if perennials are spotted. At the same time, it also enables you to spot any seedlings produced by the climber or other plants that you may want to transplant or pot up.

2 Hoeing is quicker than hand-weeding and allows you to get round more frequently. It is very effective against annual weeds but chopping the top off a perennial does not kill it and it will soon re-emerge. Do not dig too deeply with the hoe or you may disturb the roots of the plant.

3 Bark is an ideal material for mulching as it is both effective and attractive. Do not use bark that is fresh, however, or the resin may harm the plants. Hedge and shrub prunings can be shredded and used after they have been composted for a couple of months.

4 Special black polythene (plastic), with holes in it to allow water to pass through to the soil, is readily available from garden centres and nurseries. Cut the polythene to shape and lay it on the surface of the soil.

5 Polythene would be the perfect mulch if it were not so unattractive. However, it can be covered with gravel. Make certain that the polythene is flat and is completely covered with stones.

Right: *Once the planting area is covered with mulching material, the plain surface becomes the ideal background against which to see the climber.*

Watering and Feeding

Once climbers are established there is little necessity to water them, unless there are periods of extreme drought. However, it is important to water when they are first planted and while they are developing their root system.

WATERING

Lack of attention when climbers are first planted can easily kill the plants if there has not been much rain recently.

The best water to use is rain water. If possible, use water butts or tanks connected to the down-water pipe to collect water that falls on the roof of the house, garage or any other building. Tap water can be used but it is best poured first into a barrel and left to breathe before you use it. This allows time for any chlorine used in the treatment of the water to be given off.

Beware hard water that comes from chalky (alkaline) areas. Although your soil may be acidic, the water from your tap may be collected miles away, where the soil is alkaline. Hard water should not be used on ericaceous plants.

The most important aspect of watering is to always be certain to give the plants a good soaking. A sprinkle on the surface is not enough. If in doubt, dig well into the soil and see how far the moisture has penetrated through the surface.

There are several methods of watering, but a can is probably best for climbers, especially if you have only one or two. Alternatively, a hose pipe (garden hose) with a spray attachment can be used. For a large number of climbers use a sprinkler or dribble hose.

1 Give the plant a good soaking, covering the whole area around the plant where the roots will have spread. A watering can is ideal for a small area, such as around a newly planted climber that is still getting established.

2 If you have a large number of climbers or they are spread amongst shrubs and other plants, a sprinkler is a good method of providing water. To make certain that you provide sufficient water, place a jam jar or other container within the sprayed area, to give a rough idea of how much water has been delivered. It should be at least 2.5 cm (1 in) full if the watering is to do any good.

3 A spray attached to a hose pipe (garden hose) can be used as an alternative to a sprinkler. This delivers at a greater rate than a sprinkler but, even so, it must still be held in place until the ground is well and truly soaked. It is very easy to under-water using this method, as the gardener can become impatient. Freshen up the plant by spraying over the leaves, to wash away any dirt or dust.

4 A seep hose with holes in it is snaked around those plants that need to be watered and left permanently in position. It can be covered with a bark mulch, to hide it. When connected, it provides a slow dribble of water. It is an efficient method of supplying water to exactly where it is needed.

FEEDING

As well as water, a plant needs nutrients to keep healthy and to produce the maximum number of blooms. When the soil is prepared for planting, plenty of organic material should be incorporated, as well as a slow-release fertilizer. This should be sufficient for at least a year. Top-dressing in spring should provide ample nutrients. As an alternative, a general fertilizer can be applied, at the rate specified on the packet, in spring, or a liquid feed in midsummer. Do not over-feed.

2 Granular fertilizer can be applied by hand, spreading it over the area covered by the roots below. Follow the instructions on the bag.

3 Apply a layer of well-rotted organic material, such as farmyard manure or garden compost, to the surface of the soil around the plant. If the climber is not shallow-rooted, lightly fork the material into the top layer of the soil.

1 One of the easiest ways of applying fertilizer is to use a liquid feed. This can be applied during one of the regular waterings by adding it to a watering can, following the instructions on the bottle.

Right: *Walls offer perfect support and protection for climbers. Here Rosa 'Zéphirine Drouhin', Clematis 'Lady Betty Balfour' and Vitis coignettiae happily grow together.*

General Maintenance

Climbers are relatively maintenance-free and look after themselves, apart from one or two essential things. These essentials are, however, crucial not only to ensuring a good "performance" from your climbers, but also in making your garden safe for you and other users; so don't neglect these jobs, as they are important.

ESSENTIAL JOBS

The most important task is to be certain that the climber is well supported. Make regular checks that the main supports are still secure to the wall or that posts have not rotted or become loose in the wind.

Tie in any stray stems as they appear. If they are left, the wind may damage them. A worse situation can arise with thorned climbers, such as roses, whose thrashing stems may damage other plants or even passers-by. If they are not essential, cut off any stray stems to keep the climber neat and safe.

Throughout the flowering season, a climbing plant's appearance is improved by removing old flower heads. Dead-heading also prevents the plant from channelling vital resources into seed production, and thus frees energy for more flowering and growth.

WINTER PROTECTION

In winter, it may be important to protect the more tender climbers from the weather. Walls give a great deal of protection and may be sufficient for many plants but, even here, some plants may need extra protection if there is the possibility of a severe winter. One way is simply to drape hessian (burlap) or shade netting over the plant, to give temporary protection against frosts. For more prolonged periods, first protect the climber with straw and then cover this with hessian.

Keep an eye on climbers with variegated foliage, as some have the habit of reverting, that is, the leaves turn back to their normal green. If the stems bearing these leaves are not removed, the whole climber may eventually revert, losing its attractive foliage.

1 When vigorous climbers are grown against a house wall, they can become a nuisance once they have reached roof level.

4 Most climbers will produce stems that float around in space and that will need attention to prevent them being damaged or causing damage to other plants or passers-by. This *solanum* definitely needs some attention.

5 Regularly tie in any stray stems to the main supports. In some cases, it will be easier to attach them to other stems, rather than the supports. Always consider the overall shape of the climber and how you want to encourage it to grow in the future.

6 Sometimes it is better to cut off stray stems, either because there are already ample in that area or because they are becoming a nuisance. Trim them off neatly back to a bud or a branch. Sometimes, such stems will make useful cutting material from which to grow new plants.

2 At least once a year, cut back the new growth to below the level of the gutters and around the windows.

3 Dead-head regularly. If the dead flower is part of a truss, just nip out that flower; if the whole truss has finished, cut back the stem to a bud or leaf.

7 For light protection, especially against unseasonal frosts, hang shade netting or hessian (burlap) around the climber.

8 If the plant is against a wall, hang the shade netting or hessian from the gutter or from some similar support. This is a useful method of protecting new shoots and early flowers. For really tender plants, put a layer of straw around the stems of the climber and then hold it in place with a sheet of shade netting or hessian. Remove as soon as the plant begins to grow.

Above: *The overall effect of tying-in will be a neater and more satisfying shape. If possible, spread out the stems so that the climber looks fuller and less crowded.*

PRUNING

Pruning Principles

Many gardeners fight shy of attempting any form of pruning, fearing they might make a mistake and harm the plant. In fact, pruning is not as difficult as it might appear and, although you may make a few mistakes initially, it is worth persevering, because climbers will certainly benefit from attention and will eventually deteriorate if they are left to their own devices.

MAKING A GOOD CUT

One way of gaining confidence when pruning your climbers, is to learn how to make the correct cuts. Always use sharp secateurs (pruners) or a sharp saw if you are cutting larger branches. Pruning cuts should always be clean; try not to bruise or tear the wood by using worn or blunt secateurs.

Cuts to remove main stems or thick stems branching off the main stems should be made close to their origin, making certain that there is no "snag" or stump left. On the other hand the break should not be so tight that it cuts into the parent wood. Thinner stems should be cut back to a bud, leaf joint or the previous junction.

1 Make the cut just above a bud. This bud should usually be an outward-facing one, so that future growth is away from rather than towards the centre of the plant. The cut should be angled slightly away from the bud.

2 If the leaves are in pairs on the stem, one opposite the other, make the cut straight across, rather than sloping. The position should be the same, just above an outward-facing bud.

3 Always use sharp secateurs. Blunt ones will make a ragged cut and are likely to bruise the tissues, which could allow disease to enter the stem.

4 Do not cut too far above the bud. In a case like this, the stump is likely to die back, possibly causing the whole stem to rot.

5 Do not cut too close to the bud, because this might damage the bud and allow infection to enter. The stem might die back to the next bud or beyond.

6 Do not slope the cut towards the bud, because this may cause water to collect on the bud, introducing rot.

PRUNING THICK STEMS

Most stems on climbing plants can be removed with secateurs (pruners); when dealing with old wood on large climbers, however, such as some of the rambling or climbing roses, it may be necessary to use a saw.

If the stem is cut straight through, the weight from above is likely to tear the stem before the cut is complete. To prevent this, carry out the process in three stages.

1 Make a cut from the underside of the stem. Cut about half-way through or until the saw begins to bind as the weight of the stem closes the gap, pinching the saw.

2 Next, make a cut from the upper edge, this time about 2.5 cm (1 in) away from the previous cut, further away from the main stem. The weight of the stem will cause it to split across to the first cut so the main part of the branch falls to the ground.

3 Make the third cut straight through the stem at the place to which you want to cut back. This should not tear the stem, because the weight has gone.

Right: Rosa 'Bantry Bay' climbing up a metal obelisk. Roses need to be dead-headed and pruned to keep them at their best. If you don't care for them properly, the plants become very straggly and flowering diminishes.

Basic Pruning for Climbers

The basics of pruning are not at all difficult, although the task of tackling a huge climber that covers half the house may seem rather daunting. Break it into three logical stages to make it more manageable.

THREE-STAGE PRUNING

The first pruning stage is to remove all dead wood. These stems are now of no use and only make the climber congested. Moreover, clearing these first will enable you to see where to prune next.

The second stage is to remove diseased and dying wood. This type of wood is usually obvious and should be taken out before it affects the rest of the plant.

The third stage is to remove some of the older wood. This has the effect of causing the plant to throw up new growth, which ensures the plant's continuing survival and keeps it vigorous, producing plenty of healthy flowers.

DISPOSAL OF WASTE

How to get rid of the mass of waste material pruned from climbing plants has always been a problem. The traditional method was to burn it but this is a waste of organic material and creates environmental problems, especially in urban areas. The best way is to shred it (avoiding diseased material). The waste is then composted for a couple of months and then returned to the beds as a valuable mulch. If you do not own a shredder then perhaps it is possible to borrow or hire one. Some local authorities run recycling schemes in which they compost all organic garden waste for reuse. The last resort is to take it to the local refuse tip. Do not dump waste in the countryside.

PRUNING OUT DISEASED WOOD

1 Remove any diseased wood, cutting it back to a point on the stem where the wood is again healthy. If the cut end shows that the wood is still diseased on the inside of the stem, cut back further still.

REMOVING OLD WOOD

1 Up to a third of the old wood should be removed, to encourage the plant to produce new growth. If possible, cut some of this out to the base; also remove some of the upper stems, cutting them back to a strong growing point.

PRUNING OUT DEAD WOOD

1 Most climbers produce a mass of dead wood that has to be removed so that the plant does not become congested. Dead wood is normally quite clearly differentiated from the live wood, by its colour and lack of flexibility.

2 Thin out the dead wood, removing it in sections, if necessary, so that the remaining stems are not damaged when it is pulled out.

TYING IN

1 Tie in the remaining stems, spreading them out rather than tying them in a tight column of stems. If possible, spread at least some of the stems horizontally: this will not only produce a better wall or trellis cover but also encourage flowering.

Right: *At their peak, roses are amongst the loveliest of climbing plants. Here the rambling* Rosa *'Excelsa' is seen climbing up a pillar.*

Pruning Climbing Roses

Roses climbing through a tree are usually left to their own devices, because they are difficult to get at; any roses climbing up a wall, trellis or pergola, however, should be regularly pruned, not only to remove dead and old wood but also to keep them vigorous and flowering well. Unpruned roses become old before their time, their flowering decreases and they look scruffy.

ONCE-FLOWERING CLIMBING ROSES

As with most woody plants, the time to prune is immediately after flowering. For once-flowering climbing roses, this normally means in midsummer.

However, if you want to see the rose's colourful hips in the autumn, leave the pruning and wait until the birds come and remove the hips or until the fruits have lost their brilliance and are no longer attractive.

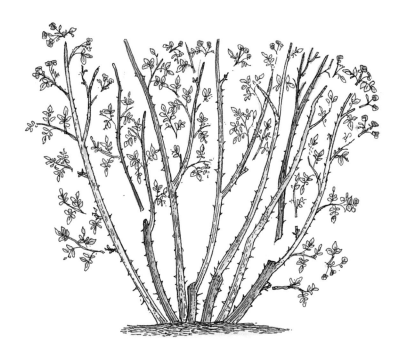

Above: *Cut out some of the older stems as soon as they have flowered, cutting back to a strong growing point, either at the base or higher up.*

1 Pruning in summer means that the plant will be in full leaf and growth. Although this may seem a daunting task to tackle, it makes it easy to see what is dead and what is alive. If possible, it is often easier to prune climbing roses by removing them from their supports and laying the stems on the ground.

2 First, remove all dead main stems and side-shoots. Cut these right back to living wood; if they are difficult to remove, take them out in sections rather than all at once. Next, remove one or two of the oldest stems. This will promote new vigorous shoots. Cut back some of the older wood growing at the top of the plant to a vigorous new shoot lower down. Do not remove more than a third of the old wood, unless you want to reduce the size of the climber drastically.

3 Tie in the remaining shoots, if they are loose. Any young shoots that come from the base will need to be regularly tied in as they grow, to prevent them from thrashing around.

4 Once secure, prune back any of the shorter side shoots to three or four buds. At the same time, cut back the tips of any new main shoots that have flowered, to a sound bud.

REPEAT-FLOWERING ROSES

There are now many roses that continue to flower throughout the summer and well into the autumn. It is obviously not desirable to prune these during the summer or you will lose the later flowers. Light pruning, restricted to removing dead flowers and any dead wood, can be carried out throughout the summer, but the main pruning is best left until the winter, when the rose is dormant. It is easier to see where to prune, too.

Below: *The abundance of flowers on Rosa 'Alba maxima' makes it impossible to prune in summer.*

REPEAT-FLOWERING ROSES

'Agatha Christie' (pink)
'Aloha' (pink)
'Bantry Bay' (pink)
'Casino' (yellow)
'Coral Dawn' (pink)
'Danse du Feu' (red)
'Gloire de Dijon' (buff)
'Golden Showers' (yellow and cream)
'Handel' (white and pink)
'Parkdirektor Riggers' (red)
'Pink Perpétue' (pink)
'Royal Gold' (yellow)
'Schoolgirl' (orange)
'Summer Wine' (pink)

1 One advantage of pruning in the winter is that the leaves are missing, giving you a clearer picture of what you are doing. The structure of the rose, in particular, is more obvious.

2 First, remove any dead or diseased wood, cutting right back into living wood. Next, take out a few of the oldest shoots from the base, to encourage new growth for a compact shape.

3 If any flowering shoots remain on the tips of the stems, cut these out, taking the stem back to a sound bud. The side shoots can be shortened to about half their length. Tie in all loose stems.

4 In the summer, dead-head the roses as the flowers go over. This not only makes the climber tidier but promotes further flowering. With tall climbers, however, this may be impractical!

Pruning Rambling Roses

Ramblers only flower once during the summer. These flowers are formed on old wood produced during the previous season, so it is important to prune as soon as possible after flowering. This allows plenty of time for new shoots to grow, ready for next season's crop of flowers.

Above: *Remove older stems as soon as they have flowered, cutting back to a strong growing point, either at the base or higher up.*

1 Because they are pruned in summer, the plants look congested and it is difficult to see what to prune. If possible, untie the shoots from their support and lay them out on the ground, so that you can see what you are doing. If this is not possible, remove the stems that need cutting out in sections and keep checking as you go.

2 Remove any diseased, dead or dying stems at the base. This may well reduce the rambler considerably and make subsequent pruning easier.

3 Cut out to the base any wood that has flowered during the summer. This should only leave new growth. However, if there is not much new growth, leave some of the older stems intact, to flower again the following season.

4 If you have retained any older shoots, cut back their side shoots to two or three buds. Tie in all remaining shoots. If possible, tie these to horizontal supports, to encourage flowering and new growth.

BARE AT THE BASE?
Sometimes rambler roses are reluctant to produce new shoots from the base of the plant. In that case, if there are new stems arising higher up the plant, cut back the old ones to this point.

Right: Rosa 'Bobby James' is a
vigorous rambling rose that
needs regular pruning to keep it
flowering well. Gloves should be
worn as it has vicious thorns.

Pruning Clematis

Many gardeners worry about pruning clematis: the task seems complex, and is made more difficult because different clematis plants require different treatment. While this is true, the actual treatment is quite simple and soon becomes routine. If you grow a lot of clematis, keep a record of which plant needs what treatment. Alternatively, attach a label to each one, stating what type it is. This will make pruning very much easier.

Above: *There is always room to grow yet another clematis. Here the double* C. viticella *'Purpurea Plena Elegans' climbs over a wooden shed. For pruning it belongs to Group 3.*

CLEMATIS PRUNING GROUPS

There are three groups of clematis, as far as pruning is concerned. Most clematis catalogues or plant labels state what type each belongs to. However, it is possible to work it out. Small-flowered spring varieties such as *Clematis montana* belong to Group 1. Several of the early-flowering species also belong to this pruning group.

Group 2 consists of large-flowered clematis that bloom in early to midsummer, on old wood produced during the previous year.

Group 3 are the large-flowered climbing plants that bloom later in the summer on new wood produced during the spring.

PRUNING GROUPS FOR SOME OF THE MORE POPULAR CLEMATIS

C. 'Abundance'	3	C. macropetala	1
C. alpina	1	C. 'Madame Julia Correvon'	3
C. 'Barbara Jackman'	2	C. 'Marie Boisselot'	2
C. 'Bill Mackenzie'	3	C. 'Miss Bateman'	2
C. cirrhosa	1	C. montana	1
C. 'Comtesse de Bouchard'	3	C. 'Mrs Cholmondeley'	2
C. 'Daniel Deronda'	2	C. 'Nelly Moser'	2
C. 'Duchess of Albany'	3	C. 'Perle d'Azur'	3
C. 'Elsa Späth'	2	C. 'Royal Velours'	3
C. 'Ernest Markham'	2	C. 'Star of India'	2
C. 'Etoile Violette'	3	C. tangutica	3
C. 'Hagley Hybrid'	3	C. tibetana (orientalis)	3
C. 'Jackmanii'	3	C. 'The President'	2
C. 'Lasurstern'	2	C. viticella	3
C. 'Little Nell'	3	C. 'Vyvyan Pennell'	2

WHICH GROUP?

Does it flower in spring or early summer and have relatively small flowers?
Yes = It is probably Group 1.
No = Go to the next question.

Does it bloom in early or midsummer, possibly with a few flowers later, and are the flowers large?
Yes = It is probably Group 2.
No = Go to the next question.

Does it flower from mid- or late summer and into autumn?
Yes = It is probably Group 3.
No = There is an area of doubt, so consult a clematis expert or specialist nursery if you cannot find the variety listed on this page.

Pruning Group 1 Clematis

This group consists mainly of small-flowered clematis. Most flower early in the year, usually in spring, such as *C. montana*, although *C. cirrhosa* flowers in winter. This is the easiest group to deal with as you can, generally, leave them to their own devices, resorting to pruning only when they grow too big and need to be cut back.

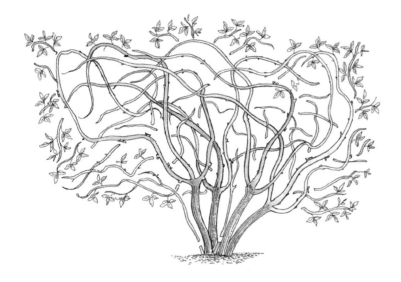

1 Keep the climber looking healthy by removing any dead growth. This will help to reduce the bulk and weight of the climber, which can become considerable over the years.

2 If space is limited, remove some stems immediately after flowering. Cut them back to where they join a main shoot. Stray shoots that are thrashing around can also be removed.

Above: *Group 1 clematis only need pruning when they outgrow their space. Just cut out sufficient branches to reduce congestion, and take those that encroach beyond their space back to their point of origin.*

Right: *Typical of Group 1 is this* C. montana.

Pruning Group 2 Clematis

Group 2 clematis need a little more care and attention to make them flower well. If they are left alone, they become very leggy, so that all the flowering is taking place at the top of the plant, out of view. The basic pruning goal is to reduce the number of shoots while leaving in a lot of the older wood. You can do this immediately after flowering but it is more usual to wait until late winter, before the clematis comes into growth.

1 First, cut out all dead or broken wood. If this is tangled up, cut it out a little at a time, so that it does not damage the wood that is to remain.

Above: *After cutting out all the dead, damaged or weak growth, remove any wood that is making the clematis congested, cutting back to a pair of buds.*

2 Cut out all weak growths, to a strong bud. If the climber is still congested, remove some of the older stems.

3 Do not remove too much material or the flowering for the following season will be reduced. If a plant has been cut back too drastically, it will often flower much later in the season than usual, and is likely to produce smaller flowers.

4 Spread out the remaining shoots, so that the support is well covered. If left to find their own way, the shoots will grow up in a column.

Right: *Correctly pruned, Group 2 clematis, such as this* Clematis *'Niobe', will provide an abundance of flowers throughout the summer.*

Pruning Group 3 Clematis

Once you have recognized that you have one of the plants that constitute this group, the actual process of pruning is very straightforward. The flowers appear on wood that grows during the current year, so all the previous year's growth can be cut away. These make good plants to grow through early-flowering shrubs, because the shrub will have finished blooming by the time that the new growth on the clematis has begun to cover its branches.

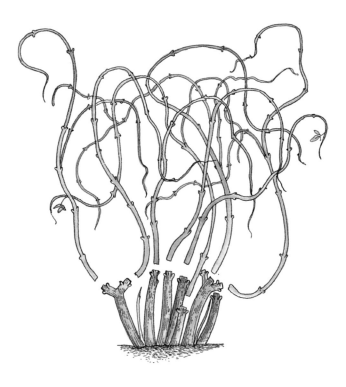

Above: *Group 3 clematis should have all the growth cut back in midwinter to the first pair of sound buds above the ground.*

1 Once Group 3 clematis become established, they produce a mass of stems at the base. If they are allowed to continue growing naturally, the flowering area gets higher and higher, leaving the base of the plant bare.

2 In mid- to late winter cut back all the shoots to within 1 m (3 ft), and preferably much less, of the ground. If the clematis is growing through a shrub, carefully untangle the stems from the shrub's branches and remove them.

3 Cut the stems back to a sound pair of plump buds. As the wood gets older, so the cuts for subsequent years are likely to get higher, but there is always plenty of new growth from the base, which should be cut low down.

4 Once cut back, the clematis looks quite mutilated but the buds will soon produce new shoots and new growth will also appear from the base; by midsummer, the support will, once again, be covered with new growth bearing a profusion of flowers.

Pruning Wisterias

Gardeners often complain that their wisteria never flowers. One of the reasons that this might happen is that they never prune the climber and consequently all the plant's energy seems to go in producing ever-expanding, new growth rather than flowers. Gardeners often seem reluctant to prune wisteria, possibly because it is usually done in two stages, one in summer and the other in winter. However, it is not at all difficult once you know the idea behind it. For the first few years allow the wisteria to grow out to form the basic framework, removing any unwanted stems.

 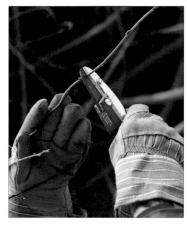

1 During the spring and early summer, the wisteria produces long, wispy new growth that looks like tendrils. Around midsummer, this new growth should be trimmed back, leaving only four leaves on each shoot. Any shoots that are required to extend the range or shape of the wisteria should be left unpruned.

2 From early to midwinter, cut back the summer-pruned shoots even further, to about half their length, leaving two to three buds on each shoot. This generally means that the previous season's growth will now be about 7.5 cm (3 in) long, thus drastically reducing the overall growth rate of the climber.

Above: *Cut back the new growth each summer to about four leaves and reduce this even further with a winter pruning.*

Right: *All the effort is worthwhile when you achieve a display as stunning as this one.*

PROPAGATING

Sowing Seed

Sowing seed is one of the easiest methods of propagation. It is also one of the most satisfying, turning what often looks like not much more than a speck of dust into a soaring plant that scrambles up the side of a house or through tall trees – it certainly gives a great sense of pleasure.

WHAT YOU WILL NEED

Sowing seed is not only a way of saving money by producing your own plants, but also one aspect of gardening that gives immense satisfaction. It is a way of producing new plants to replace ageing ones or to insure against accidental loss due to frosts or disease. It also allows the gardener to produce extra plants to give to friends or to sell. "Green fingers" are not essential – anyone can propagate climbers, as long as they follow a few well-tried principles.

There are a wide variety of different types of sowing composts (soil mixes) available and the majority of them are suitable for sowing seed of climbing plants. Unless you want to grow a huge number of one particular variety of climber, a 9 cm (3½ in) pot is a large enough container for sowing seed in; a tray (flat) will produce far too many seedlings for normal use.

As well as having the right compost and seed, for successful growing you will also need a spare pot, fine grit and plant labels, if these are available. A greenhouse or heated propagator will give the seedlings the best possible start in life.

1 Fill the pot to the rim with compost (soil mix). Tap it on the bench or table so that it settles and then *lightly* press down with the base of another pot, so that the surface is level. Do not ram the compost down into the pot.

2 Most climber seed is large, so the seeds can be sown individually with your fingers. Space the seeds out evenly over the surface, leaving well-defined gaps between them. Small seed can be scattered but, again, make certain that the seeds are thinly spread.

3 Cover the seed with 1 cm (⅓ in) of fine grit. This will make it easier to water the pot evenly as well as facilitating the removal of any weeds and moss that grow. It also provides a well-drained zone around the vulnerable neck of the seedling to prevent it from rotting.

4 Label the pot immediately; any delay may allow you to forget what seed is in which pot – all the pots tend to look the same after a few days! Put the name of the plant on the label, with the date of sowing. Keep the seed packet, if it contains any useful after-care and growing information.

5 Water the pot. Stand the pot in a sheltered position outside or in a greenhouse or a heated propagator for faster germination.

Pricking Out and Growing On Seedlings

Once the seedlings appear, it is important to keep them growing well. If you have lots of seedlings in one pot, they should not be left in their pot too long, or they will starve, which stunts their growth and makes them prone to disease. If they are overcrowded, moreover, they are likely to become drawn and spindly, so that they never develop into good healthy specimens. Use a good potting compost (soil mix) that does not contain too much fertilizer. You can use a stronger one when you pot them on at a later stage.

POTTING COMPOSTS (SOIL MIXES)

Gone are the days when every gardener had his or her own secret mixture, including all kinds of esoteric substances such as ox's blood or sheep's urine. However, there is still a baffling array of composts on offer. When all is said and done, most seem to do the job and ultimately it seems to come down to what the gardener prefers rather than the plant. The main division is between soilless and soil-based composts.

Soilless composts are mainly based on fibrous material such as peat or a peat substitute such as coir. Sometimes they contain an absorbent mineral, such as perlite or vermiculite. They are light-weight, moisture-retentive, easy to over-water and yet difficult to re-wet if allowed to dry out.

Soil-based composts are heavier, well-drained, difficult to over-water, but absorb water easily when dry.

Most composts contain varying amounts of fertilizer. For seedlings, use those with the least amount of fertilizer; for fully-grown plants, use composts with the most. Ericaceous wall shrubs, such as rhododendrons, need a special lime-free compost.

1 Fill the bottom of enough clean pots with a good potting compost (soil mix). Remove the plants, still in the compost, from the old pot. Choose a good place to split the rootball and gently divide it into two. Ease a plant away from the ball, making certain not to tear the roots. Hold the seedling by its leaves, not by the stem or roots.

2 Still holding the seedling by its leaves (avoid touching the roots), suspend it over the centre of the pot and gently surround it with compost.

3 Tap the pot on the bench, to settle the compost, and lightly firm the compost with your fingers. Level off the top of the compost and add a 1 cm (½ in) layer of fine grit, so that the surface is completely covered. At this stage, make a label to identify the plant.

4 Immediately after pricking out, water the pot thoroughly, either with a watering can with a fine rose or by standing it in a bowl of water until the surface of the grit becomes wet. Place the pot in a shady place, preferably in a closed cold-frame.

Growing from Cuttings

While using seed to increase plants is a simple procedure, it has the disadvantage that the resulting plant may not be like its parent, because not all plants will come "true" from seed. Seed-raised plants may vary in flower or leaf colour, in the size of the plant and in many other ways. When you propagate from cuttings, however, the resulting plant is identical in all ways to its parent (it is, effectively, a clone).

TAKING CUTTINGS

Taking cuttings is not a difficult procedure and nearly all climbers can easily be propagated in this way without much trouble. It is not necessary to have expensive equipment, although, if you intend to produce a lot of new plants, a heated propagator will make things much easier.

The most satisfactory method of taking cuttings is to take them from semi-ripe wood, that is, from this year's growth that is firm to the touch but still flexible and not yet hard and woody. If the shoot feels soft and floppy, it is too early to take cuttings. The best time for taking such cuttings is usually from mid- to late summer.

When taking cuttings it is vital that you always choose shoots that are healthy: they should be free from diseases and pests and not be too long between nodes (leaf joints). This usually means taking the cuttings from the top of the climber, where it receives plenty of light.

Do not take cuttings from any suckers that may rise from the base of the plant; if the climber was grafted on to a different rootstock, you might find that you have propagated another plant entirely.

CHOOSING COMPOST (SOIL MIX)

Specialist cutting compost (soil mix) can be purchased from most garden centres and nurseries. However, it is very simple to make your own. A half and half mix, by volume, of peat (or peat substitute) and sharp sand is all that is required. Alternatively, instead of sharp sand, use vermiculite.

1 Choose a healthy shoot that is not too spindly. Avoid stems that carry a flower or bud, as these are difficult to root. Cut the shoot longer than is required and trim it to size later. Put the shoot in a polythene (plastic) bag, so that it does not wilt while waiting for your attention.

2 Remove the shoot from the bag when you are ready to deal with it. Cut at an angle just below a leaf joint (node). Use a sharp knife, so that the cut is clean and not ragged.

3 Trim off the rest of the stem just above a leaf, so that the cutting is about 10 cm (4 in) long. For long-jointed climbers, this may be the next leaf joint up; for others there may be several leaves on the cutting.

4 Trim off all leaves except the upper one or pair. Cut the leaves off right against the stem, so that there are no snags. However, be careful not to damage the stem. Dip the base of the cutting into a rooting compound, either powder or liquid. This will not only promote rooting but also help protect the cutting against fungal attack.

5 Fill a 9 cm (3½ in) pot with cutting compost (soil mix) and insert the cuttings round the edge. Pushing them into the compost removes the rooting powder and damages the stems, so make a hole with a small dibber or pencil. Several cuttings can be put into one pot but do not overcrowd. Tap the pot on the bench, to settle the compost. Water gently. Label the pot.

6 If a propagator is available, place the pot in it and close the lid so that fairly high humidity and temperature are maintained. A less expensive alternative is to put the pot into a polythene (plastic) bag, with its sides held away from the leaves. Put it in a warm, light, but not sunny, position.

7 After a few weeks, the base of the cutting will callus over and roots will begin to appear. Carefully invert the pot, while supporting the compost with your other hand. Remove the pot and examine the roots. Once the roots are well developed, pot the cuttings up individually. Put the pot back in the propagator if roots are only just beginning to appear.

INTERNODAL CUTTINGS

A few plants, of which clematis is the main example, are propagated from internodal cuttings. The procedure is the same as for conventional cuttings, except that the bottom cut is through the stem, between two pairs of leaves, rather than under the bottom pair.

Right: *Your cuttings will eventually grow into hearty plants like this* Rosa *'Cedric Morris'. These rambling roses can be grown through a large tree, as long as the tree is strong enough to take all the extra weight.*

Layering

Layering is a simple technique, useful for propagating plants that are difficult to root from cuttings. It can be a slow process: occasionally, some plants can take several years to root. If one or two layers can be laid down at regular intervals, however, you should have a continuous supply of new plants at your disposal.

TIMING LAYERING

Layering can be carried out at any time of year. The time taken for roots to appear on the chosen stem depends on various factors and varies considerably from one type of plant to another. Usually, growth appearing from the area of the layer indicates that it has rooted and is ready for transplanting to another position.

ACHIEVING SUCCESS

One way of increasing the success rate with layering is to make a short slit in the underside of the stem at its lowest point. This checks the flow of the sap at this point and helps to promote rooting. Alternatively, a notch can be cut or some of the bark removed. Sometimes, just the act of forcing the stem down into a curve will wound the bark enough.

1 Make a shallow depression in the soil and place the selected stem in it. If the soil is in poor condition, remove some of it and replace it with potting compost (soil mix).

2 Use a metal pin or a piece of bent wire to hold the stem in place, if necessary, so that it cannot move in the wind.

3 Cover the stem with good soil or potting compost, and water it.

4 If you haven't pinned the stem down, place a stone on the soil above the stem, to hold it in position.

5 Once growth starts – or the stem feels as if it is firmly rooted when gently pulled – cut it away from the parent plant, ensuring that the cut is on the parent-plant side. Dig up the new plant and transfer it to a pot filled with potting compost. Alternatively, replant it elsewhere in the garden.

6 An alternative method is to insert the layer directly into a pot of compost, which is buried in the ground. Once the stem has rooted, sever it from the parent as above and dig up the whole pot. This is a good technique for making tip layers, as with this fruit-bearing tayberry. Tip layers are made by inserting the tip of a stem, rather than a central section, in the ground, until it roots; it is a suitable propagation technique for fruiting climbers, such as blackberries.

Right: *Roses are just one of the types of climber that can be propagated by layering.*

TYPES OF CLIMBERS

Annual Climbers

When considering climbers, most gardeners automatically think of woody climbing plants, such as clematis or roses, and forget about the annuals. However, annual climbers are extremely useful plants and should never be overlooked.

INSTANT COLOUR

One of the great virtues of annual climbers is that they are temporary; they allow the gardener the opportunity of changing the plants or changing their position every year. This means that it is possible to fill gaps at short notice or simply to change your mind as to the way the garden should look.

Another virtue of annuals is that they come in a wide range of colours, some of which are not so readily available in other climbers. The "hot" colours – red, orange, yellow – in particular, are of great use. Annuals, on the whole, have a very long flowering season, much longer than most perennials. This also makes them very useful.

The one drawback of annuals is that they must be raised afresh each year. Many can be bought as young plants from garden centres but all can be raised from seed. This doesn't require a lot of time or space: the majority will germinate quite happily on a kitchen windowsill. With the exception of sweet peas, which are hardy and should be sown in winter, most annuals should be sown in spring, pricked out into pots, hardened off and then planted out in the open ground as soon as the threat of frosts has passed.

Annuals can be grown up any type of support, both permanent and temporary. Although they are only in place for a few months, some, such as *Cobaea scandens* (cathedral bells), can cover a very large area. Nasturtiums (*Tropaeolum*) are also annuals that can put on a lot of growth in a season.

Above: *Many climbers can be used as trailing plants as well as climbing ones. Annual nasturtiums are a good example of this. Here the nasturtium 'Jewel of Africa' is seen around a purple-leaved* Canna *'Wyoming'.*

Above: *Not all "annuals" are strictly annual.* Eccremocarpus scaber, *shown here, is really a perennial but it is often treated as an annual and planted afresh every year. It is shown with an everlasting pea,* Lathyrus latifolius.

Above: *Annuals are not restricted to just flowers. Many vegetables also make attractive climbers as well as being productive. Here, scarlet runner beans are grown up a wigwam (tepee) of canes. This is not only attractive but allows the gardener to produce quite a large crop in a small space.*

Above: *Sweet peas are amongst everyone's favourite climbers. Not only do they look good in the garden; they are also wonderful flowers for cutting for the house. Most have a delicious scent.*

Right: Cobaea scandens *is a vigorous annual climber. For success it must be planted in a warm position, preferably against a wall, and given as long a growing season as possible.*

Left: *The morning glories,* Ipomoea, *are just that, glorious. Soak seeds overnight before sowing and germinate in a warm place or propagator. Harden off thoroughly before planting or they are unlikely to do well. Plant them in a sheltered sunny position.*

Evergreen Climbers

Climbing plants are mainly valued for their flowers, but there are a few that hold their place in the garden because of their evergreen foliage. Probably the best known is ivy. Its glossy, three-pointed leaves make a permanent cover for whatever they climb up.

FOLIAGE SCREENS

One of the best uses of evergreens is as a cover for eyesores. They can be grown directly over an ugly wall or allowed to clamber over trellising judiciously positioned to hide a fuel tank or messy utility area. There are some places in the garden, moreover, where it is preferable that the appearance does not change with the seasons. A gateway, perhaps, may be surrounded by an evergreen climber over an arch, so that it presents the same familiar image to the visitor all year round.

From a design point of view, evergreen climbers provide a permanent point of reference within the garden. They form part of the structure, around which the rest of the garden changes season by season.

Plain green can be a little uninspiring; green works extremely well, however, as a backdrop against which to see other, more colourful, plants. Climbers such as ivy have glossy leaves, which reflect the light, giving a shimmering effect as they move. Evergreen leaves can vary in shape, and they can also be variegated, providing contrasting tones of green and sometimes colour variation.

Right: Laurus nobilis *provides attractive green foliage.*

EVERGREEN CLIMBERS
Clematis armandii
Clematis cirrhosa
Fremontodendron
   californicum
Hedera (ivy)
Lonicera japonica
Solanum crispum
Solanum jasminoides
Vinca major (periwinkle)

EVERGREEN WALL SHRUBS
Azara
Callistemon citrinus
Carpenteria californica
Ceanothus
Coronilla glauca
Cotoneaster
Desfontainea spinosa
Elaeagnus x ebbingei
Elaeagnus pungens
Escallonia
Euonymus fortunei
Euonymus japonicus
Garrya elliptica
Itea ilicifolia
Laurus nobilis
Magnolia grandiflora
Piptanthus laburnifolius
Pyracantha (firethorn)
Teucrium fruticans

Above: *Variegated ivies can make a big impact. Those with golden variegation are excellent for lighting up dark corners and they are especially good in helping to brighten the grey days of winter.*

Above: *Although the flowers of ivy are insignificant, the evergreen leaves make a valuable contribution to the garden. Here, three different varieties make a dense screen.*

Right: *This* Solanum crispum *'Glasnevin' is one of the very best climbers. Unless the weather gets very cold, it retains its shiny leaves throughout the winter and then is covered with its blue flowers from late spring right through to the autumn. The leaves may drop during severe winters, but they soon recover.*

Above: Vinca major *(periwinkle) can be considered a shrub if it is kept rigorously under control by cutting back, but it is often used as a climber, scrambling through shrubs and hedges, as here. It retains its glossy green leaves throughout the winter and produces bright blue flowers from midwinter onwards.*

Below: *There is a brightly variegated periwinkle, 'Variegata', which looks good against dark hedges.*

Climbers with Spring Interest

Spring is one of the most joyous times of the year in the garden; the winter is over and ahead lie the glories of summer. Many of the plants that flower at this time of year have a freshness about them that almost defies definition.

PROTECTING FROM FROST

Spring is a time of varying weather and plants can suffer badly from late frosts. This is made worse when frosts are preceded by a warm spell, in which a lot of new growth appears. These young shoots are susceptible to sudden cold weather and can be burnt off. Buds are also likely to be harmed and it is not uncommon to see a *Clematis montana*, for example, covered in buds and full of promise one day, only to be denuded of buds the next after a night of hard frost. This, however, should never deter you from growing spring-flowering climbers; such frosts do not occur every year and, in most springs, these climbers perform at their best. If frosts are forecast, it is possible to guard against them.

Many of the more tender early-flowering shrubs need walls for protection and are usually grown as wall shrubs. Shrubs such as camellias are particularly prone to frost damage and so are grown in this way.

Once they have finished flowering, many spring-flowering climbers are a bit dreary for the rest of the year. One way to enliven them is to grow another, later-flowering, climber through their stems. This is very useful where space is limited.

SPRING-FLOWERING CLIMBERS AND WALL SHRUBS

Abeliophyllum distichum
Akebia quinata
Akebia trifoliata
Azara serrata
Ceanothus arboreus 'Trewithen Blue'
Chaenomeles (japonica or ornamental quince)
Clematis alpina
Clematis armandii
Clematis macropetala
Clematis montana
Forsythia suspensa
Garrya elliptica
Lonicera (honeysuckles)
Piptanthus laburnifolius
Ribes laurifolia
Rosa (early roses)
Schisandra
Solanum cripsum 'Glasnevin'
Wisteria

Above: *Spring is the time when all plants are beginning to burst forth. Clematis are some of the earliest climbers, one of the earliest and most impressive being* C. montana, *which frequently has so much bloom that the leaves cannot be seen.*

Right: Clematis armandii *is one of the few evergreen clematis. It is also one of the earliest to flower, doing so in late winter or early spring.*

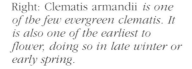

Above: *Another early clematis, more delicate in appearance, is* C. macropetala. *It is here seen with* C. montana, *which will flower a week or so later.*

Above: *Honeysuckles (*Lonicera*) are a great feature of the spring. This one (*L. periclymenum*) is in a natural habitat – scrambling through a bush. In this case, the supporting plant is a berberis, whose purply-bronze leaves make a good contrast to the yellow flowers.*

Left: Rosa *'Maigold' is one of the many roses that although strictly a shrub, have a tendency to climb. They can be used as low climbers up pillars, as here, or on tripods, trellis or low walls. It starts flowering early in the season and often repeats later in the year.*

Right: *When in full flower, wisteria must be one of the most beautiful of climbers. It can be grown as a free-standing tree but it is best supported on a wall or pergola. Walls help to protect it against late frosts which can damage the flower buds.*

Climbers with Summer Interest

Summer is when many climbers are at their best. Clematis and roses, in particular, produce plenty of blooms, covering pergolas and arches as well as climbing up walls and through trees and shrubs. They make a valuable contribution to the summer scene, giving vertical emphasis to a garden that would otherwise be flat and less interesting.

SUMMER CLIMBERS

Campsis	*Phaseolus coccineus* (runner
Clematis	beans)
Cobaea scandens (cathedral	*Plumbago auriculata* (Cape
bells)	leadwort)
Eccremocarpus scaber (Chilean	*Rosa* (roses)
glory flower)	*Schisandra*
Fallopia baldschuanica	*Schizophragma*
(Russian vine)	*Solanum crispum*
Ipomoea (morning glories)	'Glasnevin'
Jasminum (jasmines)	*Solanum jasminoides*
Lapageria rosea	*Thunbergia alata* (black-eyed
Lathyrus (peas)	Susan)
Lonicera (honeysuckles)	*Trachelospermum*
Mutisia	*Tropaeolum* (nasturtium)
Passiflora (passion-flowers)	*Wisteria*

SHADE AND FRAGRANCE

During hot, sunny summers, climbers are most welcome for providing dappled shade as they cover arbours and pergolas. There is nothing better than to sit on a summer's day in the shade of an arbour or relax there with a meal or a drink in the evening after work. Relaxation is further enhanced if the climbers are fragrant – and many are. Roses, honeysuckle and jasmine are three of the most popular scented climbers.

Many shrubs and trees are spring-flowering and climbers can be used to enliven them during the summer months, when they are, perhaps, at their dullest. *Clematis viticella* is probably the best to use for this purpose; because it is cut back almost to the ground during the winter, it doesn't smother the tree or shrub when it is in flower. Later in the season, when the tree or shrub has finished flowering, the clematis grows up through its branches and produces its own colour, usually over a long period.

Similarly, climbers can be used in herbaceous borders, where there are gaps left by perennials that flower early in the season and are then cut back. Clematis can be left to scramble through the border, either without any support or over a simple framework of twigs.

Above: Campsis radicans *is a beautiful climber for the second half of the summer. Its large tubular flowers, here just opening, contrast well with the green of the foliage. It is not a common climber but it is not difficult to find or to grow.*

Above: Clematis florida *'Sieboldii' is a very distinct clematis, with creamy white outer petals and an inner button of purple ones. It is a beautiful flower even when still in bud and while opening.*

Right: Clematis *'Perle d'Azur' must be one of the best of the blue clematis. It produces flowers of a delicate lilac blue in tremendous profusion around midsummer.*

Above: *Bougainvillea is a climber from hot climates. In more temperate areas, it has to be grown under glass, such as in a conservatory, but, in warmer districts, it can be grown outside. Its brilliant colours continue for months as it is the papery bracts rather than the flowers that provide the colour.*

Right: *Scrambling plants are a neglected area. There are very many of them and they can provide a lot of vertical interest through the summer months. Here a* Euonymus fortunei *'Emerald Gaiety' scrambles up through a large bush, with* Geranium x oxonianum *pushing its way up through both.*

Left: *Unlike the sweet pea, the perennial* Lathyrus grandiflorus *does not smell, but it is a most beautiful small climber. The round pea flowers are large and full of rich colour. They are best planted under shrubs, through which they will happily scramble.*

Above: *Another scrambler is* Tropaeolum speciosum. *This, like* Lathyrus grandiflorus, above, *has a more common annual relative, the nasturtium. However,* Tropaeolum speciosum *is a perennial and has small flowers of an intense flame red. It will scramble up through any shrub.*

Right: Tropaeolum peregrinum *(canary creeper) is tender to frosts, but if protected will flower throughout the summer.*

Left: *Not all climbers need to climb to great heights to be attractive. This herbaceous climber scrambles up through other plants with gay abandon. It is* Convolvulus althaeoides *and has delicate pink flowers, which are set off well against its silver foliage. It likes a sunny, well-drained spot.*

Above: *Passion-flowers are tender climbers, best grown against walls. Most should be grown under glass but* Passiflora caerulea *is hardy enough to be grown outside. The flowers are amongst the most extraordinary of all climbers.*

Right: *For many people, roses are the best summer climbing plants. They can be grown in a wide variety of ways, including up tripods, as seen here. This is* Rosa *'Dortmund'.*

Climbers with Autumn Interest

Most climbers have finished flowering by the time the autumn arrives but many have qualities that make them still desirable in the garden at this time of year.

FOLIAGE AND BERRIES

Perhaps the biggest attraction of autumn climbers is the change in colour of the leaves, prior to their fall. Many take on autumnal tints, some of the most fiery red. This will completely transform the appearance of the climber itself and, often, that of the surrounding area. Another benefit that some climbers have to offer is that they produce berries or fruit. Most produce seed of some kind or other but these are often visually insignificant; others produce an abundance of bright berries – honeysuckle (*Lonicera*), for example – or large luxurious fruit, such as the passion-flowers (*Passiflora*). Others carry their seeds in a different but, none the less, very attractive way. The fluffy or silky seed heads of clematis, for example, always make an interesting feature.

As well as providing an important visual element in the garden, the berries and other forms of seed are also a good source of food for birds. Birds will be attracted to the fruit for as long as they last, which may be well beyond the autumn and into the winter. Not only birds like fruit: man also likes the garden's edible bounty and many fruiting plants, ranging from currants and gooseberries to apples, plums, pears and apricots, can be grown against a wall, which provides not only support but also warmth and protection. Fruiting trees, such as apples and pears, also make good plants to train up and over arches and pergolas.

Right: Pyracantha *offers the choice of yellow, red or orange berries, depending on the variety. This is* P. *'Orange Charmer'.*

AUTUMNAL-FOLIAGED CLIMBERS

Actinidia (kiwi fruit)
Akebia quinata
Campsis
Chaenomeles (japonica or flowering quince)
Clematis alpina
Clematis flammula
Clematis tibetana vernayi
Cotoneaster
Fallopia baldschuanica (Russian vine)
Hydrangea anomala petiolaris
Hydrangea aspera
Hydrangea quercifolia
Jasminum officinale (jasmine)
Lonicera tragophylla (honeysuckle)
Parthenocissus (Boston ivy or Virginia creeper)
Passiflora (passion-flower)
Ribes speciosum
Rosa (roses)
Tropaeolum (nasturtium)
Vitis (grapevine)

BERRIED AND FRUITING CLIMBERS AND WALL SHRUBS

Actinidia (kiwi fruit)
Akebia
Clematis
Cotoneaster
Hedera (ivy)
Humulus lupulus (hop)
Ilex (holly)
Lonicera (honeysuckle)
Malus (crab apple)
Passiflora (passion-flower)
Prunus (plums, apricots, peaches)
Pyracantha (firethorn)
Pyrus (pears)
Rosa (roses)
Vitis (grapevine)

Above: Clematis cirrhosa *flowers in late autumn and carries its fluffy seed heads well into winter.*

Left: *The berries of* Cotoneaster horizontalis *are set off well against the foliage of* Helleborus foetidus.

Above and right: Parthenocissus henryana *is seen here in both its summer and autumn colours.*

Left: *Clematis display a mass of silky heads as beautiful as any flowers throughout the autumn.*

Below: *Fruit trees are attractive as wall shrubs as they carry blossom in spring and fruit in the autumn. This pear, 'Doyenne du Comice', has attractive foliage, too.*

Climbers with Winter Interest

While there are not many climbers that are interesting in winter, they are still a group of plants that are worth thinking about. Valuable wall space should not be taken up with plants that do not earn their keep for the greater part of the year, but it is often possible to find space for at least one that brightens up the winter scene.

WINTER-FLOWERING CLIMBERS
Surprisingly, there is one clematis that is in full flower during the bleaker winter months. *Clematis cirrhosa* is available in several forms, some with red blotches on their bell-shaped flowers. *Clematis armandii* appears towards the end of winter and heralds the beginning of a new season. There are three honeysuckles that flower in the winter and, although they are, strictly speaking, shrubs, they can be grown against a wall. As an added bonus, these are very strongly scented and they will flower throughout the whole of

the winter. Another wall shrub that flowers early is *Garrya elliptica*, with its long, silver catkins. This is the more valuable because it will grow on a north-facing wall.

One of the most commonly grown wall shrubs is the winter jasmine, *Jasminum nudiflorum*, which produces a wonderful display of bright yellow flowers. Unfortunately, unlike its summer relatives, it is not scented.

EVERGREEN CLIMBERS
While not so attractive as the flowering plants, evergreen climbers, such as ivy (*Hedera*), can be used as winter cover both for walls and for other supports. These evergreen climbers afford valuable winter protection for birds and insects, especially if grown by a warm wall. Different green tones and, especially, variegated leaves, can add a surprising amount of winter cheer, even on dark days.

Climbers and wall shrubs that still carry berries from the previous autumn can add interest in the winter. Cotoneaster and pyracantha are good examples.

Above: Hedera colchica *'Dentata Variegata' is in perfect condition even in these frosty conditions. The gold variegation is good for lightening up dark winter days.*

Above: *The winter jasmine,* Jasminum nudiflorum, *flowers throughout winter, supplying cut flowers for indoors and decorating walls and fences outside.*

Right: Clematis armandii *flowers in late winter, with a wonderful display of pure-white flowers.*

WINTER CLIMBERS AND WALL SHRUBS
Chaenomeles (japonica or flowering quince)
Clematis armandii
Clematis cirrhosa
Elaeagnus x ebbingei
Elaeagnus pungens
Garrya elliptica
Hedera (ivy)
Jasminum nudiflorum (winter jasmine)
Lonicera fragrantissima (winter honeysuckle)
Lonicera x purpusii
Lonicera standishii

Above: Garrya elliptica *is an excellent plant for winter. It has beautiful silver catkins and is one of the few plants suitable for growing on north-facing walls.*

Above: Clematis cirrhosa *is the earliest clematis to flower, starting in early winter and continuing until spring. The many varieties include this one, 'Balearica'.*

Right: Chaenomeles, *known as* japonica, *or Japanese or ornamental quince, flowers from midwinter to spring, then has hard fruit that often lasts through until the next spring.*

Fragrant Climbers

When choosing plants, the main consideration is, often, what the flowers are like, followed by the foliage. Something that is often forgotten, or just considered as a bonus, is fragrance; and yet it is something that most people enjoy and it enhances the pleasure of all uses of the garden.

USING FRAGRANCE

Climbers include some of the loveliest and most scented plants in the garden. Some of them, such as honeysuckle or jasmine, will perfume the air over a long distance. They are always worth growing on house walls near windows that are often open, so that the beautiful smells waft in and fill the rooms. Another good place to locate fragrant climbers is over an arbour or where there is a seat. Fragrance can be a tremendous aid to relaxation: just think about the idea of sitting in the evening, after a hard day, with the air filled with the smell of honeysuckle, for example.

Most scented climbers are at their best in the evening. This is a bonus if you are at work all day and, again, makes them very suitable for planting where you relax or have your evening meal. Some scented climbers, such as sweet peas, make ideal flowers for cutting to bring indoors.

Check carefully that a climber is fragrant. Honeysuckles (*Lonicera*) are amongst the most fragrant of climbers, but not all of them are scented, by any means. *Lonicera tragophylla* and *L. × tellmanniana* are both very attractive honeysuckles, but neither has any smell at all. Roses, too, vary in the intensity of their scent, and it is worth finding out which ones you like best. Another thing to be beware of is that not all smells are nice. The privets (*Ligustrum*), which are sometimes used as wall shrubs, have a smell that many people find revolting.

FRAGRANT CLIMBERS AND WALL SHRUBS

Azara
Clematis montana
Itea ilicifolia
Jasminum (jasmine)
Lathyrus odoratus
   (sweet peas)
Lonicera (honeysuckle)
Magnolia grandiflora
Osmanthus
Passiflora (passion-flower)
Rosa (roses)

Above: *The fragrance of this* Rosa '*Wedding Day' climbing through a tree will be carried far in the warm summer evenings.*

Above: *Honeysuckle has a very heady perfume, from flowers that first appear in spring and then continue through the summer; odd flowers are still being produced in autumn.*

Left: *Not all honeysuckles are fragrant but* Lonicera periclymenum *and its varieties are amongst the best. They can be vigorous growers and need strong supports.*

Above: *Growing* Rosa *'Zéphirine Drouhin' around a summer house is ideal. This rose has a delightful perfume and flowers on and off throughout the summer and well into the autumn. It has the advantage that it is thornless and so is safe to use near places where people are sitting or walking.*

Above: *Jasmine has a very distinctive fragrance and is most appreciated on a warm summer evening. This variety,* Jasminum officinale *'Aureum', has gold-splashed leaves. This gives the climber an attraction even when it is out of flower.*

Right: *Roses grown on walls next to windows will fill the adjoining rooms with relaxing perfumes. Here* Rosa *'Iceberg' and* Rosa *'Albertine' mingle colour and fragrance near a bedroom window.*

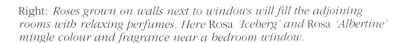

Wall Shrubs

Not all plants that one sees climbing up walls or supported on trellis are true climbers. Many are just ordinary shrubs that are growing against a wall for a variety of reasons. In the wild, some of these might scramble through others if they are next to them, but, generally, they are free-standing shrubs. These shrubs are used as surrogate climbers in the garden, partly because they look good in positions where climbers are grown and partly because some need the protection that walls and fences provide.

WALL SHRUBS

Abutilon	*Ficus carica* (fig)
Azara	*Fremontodendron californicum*
Carpenteria californica	(fremontia)
Ceanothus (Californian lilac)	*Garrya elliptica*
Chaenomeles (japonica,	*Itea ilicifolia*
ornamental quince)	*Jasminum* (jasmine)
Clianthus puniceus	*Magnolia*
(parrot's bill)	*Pyracantha* (firethorn)
Cotoneaster	*Teucrium fruticans*
Euonymus fortunei	(shrubby germander)

ADVANTAGES OF WALL SHRUBS

From the design point of view, wall shrubs are often more compact and controllable than climbers. They can be used in smaller spaces, which climbers would soon outgrow. If so desired, they can be clipped into topiary shapes and they will retain their shape for some time, unlike climbers, which have a constant tendency to throw out new shoots. Wall shrubs increase the range of flowering colours and periods available to the gardener, as well as offering a greater range of foliage effects.

Walls offer winter protection to many shrubs that could otherwise not be grown. The warmth that comes from a house wall might horrify the conservationally minded but, to the gardener, it offers the opportunity to grow plants, such as *Ceanothus*, which might otherwise succumb to the cold weather and die.

It is sometimes difficult to tell what is a climber and what is a wall shrub. *Pyracantha* cut tight against a wall, for example, has every appearance of being a climber, as has a large *Magnolia grandiflora*. *Euonymus fortunei*,

which grows like any other shrub in the open ground, will, given the chance, shin up a wall as if that were its normal habitat. But, in fact, the difference between climbers and wall shrubs does not matter. Most gardeners are concerned about the appearance of the garden and are not worried about categories. Sad would be the case if a plant were banished from a wall or some other support simply because it was not, strictly speaking, a climber.

Above: Piptanthus nepalensis *blooms in the spring, producing bright yellow, pea-like flowers. As summer moves on, so these attractive pods are formed, adding yet another dimension to the plant. Both the flowers and pods show up well against a brick wall.*

Left: Fremontodendron californicum *is usually grown against a wall. Wear a mask when pruning or handling as the stems are covered with fine hairs that can get into the lungs.*

Right: *Although most frequently used as a free-standing shrub,* Euonymus fortunei *'Emerald 'n' Gold' will happily climb up a wall or fence.*

Above: Carpenteria californica *is one of the glories of the summer, with its large white flowers, surmounted by a boss of yellow stamens. These are set off well by the dark green foliage. This plant is usually grown as a wall shrub, because it is slightly tender and appreciates the protection of the wall.*

Left: Calistemon citrinus, *with its curious, bottle-brush-like flowers, is a tender shrub that needs the warm protection of a wall if it is to survive. It flowers during the summer months.*

Above: Ceanothus *produces some of the best blue flowers of any wall shrubs. Many can be grown free-standing, but most do best if grown against a wall or a fence as here.*

TRAINING CLIMBERS

Training Methods 1

Training is an important aspect of growing climbers. The general shape and well-being of the plant is taken care of by pruning, but how it is trained and where it is positioned are the most important things to consider when thinking about how your climber will look.

POSITIONING THE PLANT

The overall shape of the plant depends on its position. Those against a wall, for example, need to be tied in so that they do not protrude too far. Similarly, climbers over arches must be constrained on at least the inner side, so that they do not catch people walking through the arch. In some places, the plants can be left to show off the way they froth out over their supports. Vigorous climbers covering large trees, for example, are best left natural and untrained. Plants on trellis can be allowed a certain amount of ebullient freedom but they may also need some restraint.

SPREADING OUT THE STEMS

The climber's natural tendency is to go straight up through its support or host until it reaches the light. This frequently means that the climber forms a tight column without much deviation on either side. To make a good display the gardener should spread out the stems at as early a stage as possible so that the main stems fan out, covering the wall, fence or trellis. This not only means that the climber covers a wider area but also that its stems all receive a good amount of light, and thus flowering is encouraged at a lower level.

EARLY DAYS

At the time of planting it can be a good policy to train individual stems along canes until they reach the wires, trellis or whatever the support may be. This will prevent them from all clustering together, making it difficult to train them at a later stage. Once the plant starts to put on growth, tie this in rather than tucking it behind the trellis or wires. This will enable you to release it at a later stage to re-organize it.

Above: *Tying in climbers under overhanging tiles can be a problem, because it may be difficult to find anchor points. A criss-cross arrangement of vertical wires can normally be fixed between the end of the eaves and the wall below the tiles; it makes an attractive feature in its own right. Here,* Rosa *'Zéphirine Drouhin' is supported on wires.*

Right: *Horizontal training produces some of the best flowering. Here,* Rosa *'Seagull' has been trained along swags of rope suspended between wooden pillars. Do not pull the ropes too tight: a graceful curve gives a much better effect. If it is not self-clinging, tie the climber in well to the rope or it will become loose and thrash about.*

Above: *A similar effect to climbing on ropes can be had by training the climber along poles attached to pillars. These form a rustic trellis and can look very effective, even during the winter when the climber is not in leaf. Here, Rosa 'Felicia' clambers over the structure.*

Right: *Vigorous climbers, such as rambling roses, some clematis and Russian vines, can be grown through trees. This is an easy way of training because, once the plant has been pointed in the right direction (by tying it to a cane angled into the tree), it can be left to its own devices. Make certain that the tree can support the weight of the climber, especially in high winds. Here Rosa 'Paul's Himalayan Musk' begins its ascent.*

Training Methods 2

ENCOURAGING FLOWERS

Once the climber has thrown up some nice long shoots, bend these over in a curving arc and attach them to the wires or trellis. From these will come new shoots which should be treated in the same manner so that the wall, fence or trellis is covered in a increasing series of arching stems. This method has the advantage, besides creating a good coverage of the wall, of making the plant produce plenty of flowers. The chemistry of the stems is such that flower buds are laid down on the top edge of the curving branches. Roses, in particular, benefit greatly from this method of training.

Curving branches over to encourage growth can also be used for climbers growing around tripods or round a series of hooped sticks, where the stems are tied around the structure rather than in a vertical position. This will encourage a much thicker coverage and many more blooms as well as allowing you to use vigorous plants in a limited amount of space.

CHOOSING YOUR METHOD OF TRAINING

There are endless possibilities for training your climber, and really the choice will affected by the constraints of the garden and personal choice. You may have something particular in mind – for example, you may want to construct a shady arbour or romantic walkway – or you may have simply bought a climber you took a fancy to and now want to find a good place for it where it will flourish and add to the beauty of the garden.

TRAINING CLIMBERS OVER EYESORES

Climbers that grow quickly and produce lots of flowers are well-suited to covering unsightly features in the garden such as refuse areas, grey concrete walls belonging to a neighbouring property or ugly fences you are not allowed to pull down.

CLIMBERS TO TRAIN OVER EYESORES

Clematis montana
Clematis rehderiana
Fallopia baldschuanica (Russian vine)
Hedera (ivy)
Humulus (hops)
Hydrangea anomala petiolaris
Lonicera (honeysuckles)
Rosa (roses)

CLIMBERS AND WALL SHRUBS FOR NORTH- AND EAST-FACING WALLS

Akebia quinata
Camellia
Chaenomeles (Japonica or ornamental quince)
Clematis 'Marie Boisselot'
Clematis 'Nelly Moser'
Euonymous fortunei
Jasminum nudiflorum
Hedera (Ivy)
Hydrangea anomala petiolaris
Lonicera x tellemanniana
Parthenocissus (Boston ivy or virginia creeper)
Pyracantha (Firethorn)
Rosa 'New Dawn'
Schizophragma

Above: Rosa *'New Dawn'* has a very long flowering period and has the added benefit that it can be grown on a north-facing wall. Here it has been tied into trellising on a wall.

Left: *Climbers planted near doorways should be kept under control to avoid injury. Clematis, such as this C. 'Rouge Cardinal', are safer than roses as they have no thorns to catch the unwary.*

Above: *When roses are well-trained they can produce an abundance of flowers. The curiously coloured R. 'Veilchenblau', shown here growing up a wooden trellis, puts on a fine show during midsummer.*

Above: *If possible, train climbers that have scented flowers near open windows, so that their fragrance can be appreciated indoors. Here Rosa 'Albertine' is in full flower, while beyond is a wisteria that has finished flowering.*

Right: *To obtain extra height for the more vigorous roses a trellis can be erected on top of a wall. When well-trained they present a backdrop of colour against which to view the border in front and below.*

Growing Climbers on Wires

If a large area of wall is to be covered with non-clinging climbers, wires are the only realistic way of supporting them. Alternative methods, such as covering the whole wall with wooden trellis, are expensive and, if the wall is at all attractive, may detract from its appearance.

HOW TO USE WIRES

Wires can be used for most types of climbers, except for clinging ones, which should be able to cling directly to the surface of the wall. If the wires are too far apart, however, plants with tendrils may have difficulty finding the next wire up and may need to be tied in. Wires are also suitable for wall shrubs, which while not needing support, benefit from being tied in to prevent them from being blown forward by wind rebounding from the wall. Wires are unobtrusive and can be painted the same colour as the wall, to make them even less visible. Galvanized wire is best, as it will not rust. Rusty wires are not only liable to break but may also cause unsightly rust marks that may show up on the wall. Plastic-covered wire can be used but the coating is not as permanent as a galvanized one.

Do not use too thin a wire or it will stretch under the weight of the plants. If there is a chance that the wires will stretch, use bottle screws or tension bolts at one end. These can be tightened as the wire slackens.

1 Before it is fixed to wires, the young plant is loose and growing in all directions.

2 The wires are supported by vine eyes, which are fastened into the wall. Although you might be able to hammer them directly into soft brickwork, it is usually easier to drill a pilot hole.

3 If you are using vine eyes with a screw fixing, you need to insert a plastic or wooden plug in the wall first. The eye is then screwed into the plug. This type of vine eye varies in length, the long ones being necessary for those climbers, such as wisteria, that grow large and need wires further from the wall.

4 The simplest vine eyes are wedge shaped. Hammer them directly into the masonry and then feed the wire through a hole. While wedge-shaped eyes are suitable for brick and stone walls, the screw type are better for wooden fences and posts.

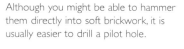

5 Thread the galvanized wire through the hole in the vine eye and wrap it round itself, forming a firm fixing. Thread the other end through the intermediate eyes (set at no more than 180 cm/6 ft intervals and preferably closer) and then fasten the wire round the end eye, keeping it as taut as possible.

6 Curve over the long stems and attach them to the wires, using either plastic ties or string. Tie at several points, if necessary, so that the stems lie flat against the wall and do not flap about.

7 When all the stems are tied in, you should have a series of arches. Tying them in like this, rather than straight up the wall, covers the wall better and encourages the plant to produce flowering buds all along the top edge of the stems.

Above: *Climbers such as roses and clematis can be trained up the whole side of a house with wires. Here* Rosa *'Madame Isaac Pereire' completely covers its wires.*

Fixing Trellis to Walls

Permanent wooden trellis, fixed to a wall, is not only a strong method of supporting climbers but also an attractive one. However, large areas of trellis can look overpowering, especially on house walls; wires are a better choice for these situations. Apart from self-clinging plants, which support themselves, any type of climber can be held up by such trellis.

HOW TO USE TRELLIS

The trellis should be well fixed to the wall, preferably with screws. It should be held a short distance from the brickwork or masonry, so that the stems of the climber can easily pass up behind it. This can be simply achieved by using spacers – wooden blocks will do – between the trellis and the wall.

If the wall is a painted one, or might need future attention for other reasons, it is possible to make the trellis detachable. The best method is to fix hinges along the bottom edge of the trellis. This allows the framework to be gently eased away from the wall, bringing the climber with it, so that maintenance can

take place. The top is held by a catch. Alternatively, the trellis can be held in position by a series of clips or catches. This is not so easy to manoeuvre as one held on hinges, however.

Any shape of trellis can be used, such as square, rectangular or fan shaped, depending on the climber and the effect of the shape on the building or wall. It is possible to be more imaginative and devise other shapes, perhaps creating a two-dimensional topiary. The mesh can be either square or diagonal, the former being better with brickwork, because the lines of the trellis then follow those of the brick courses rather than contradicting them.

CLIMBERS FOR TRELLIS

Akebia
Clematis
Cobaea scandens (cathedral bells)
Humulus (hop)
Ipomoea (morning glory)
Lathyrus odoratus (sweet peas)
Lonicera (honeysuckle)
Rosa (roses)
Solanum crispum
Solanum jasminoides
Thunbergia alata (black-eyed Susan)

1 Take the trellis to the wall and mark its position. Drill holes for fixing the spacers and insert plastic or wooden plugs.

2 Drill the equivalent holes in the wooden batten and secure it to the wall, checking with a spirit level that it is horizontal. Use a piece of wood that holds the trellis at least 2.5 cm (1 in) from the wall. Fix a similar batten at the base and one half-way up for trellis above 1.2 m (4 ft) high.

3 Drill and screw the trellis to the battens, first fixing the top and then working downwards. Check that the trellis is not crooked.

4 The finished trellis should be tightly fixed to the wall, so that the weight of the climber, and any wind that blows on it, will not pull it away from its fixings.

Above: *The rose 'Dublin Bay' here climbs up a wooden trellis secured to the wall. This rose is fragrant and flowers over a very long period.*

Growing Climbers on Netting

A cheap but effective method of providing support for climbers on a wall is to use a rigid plastic netting. This can be used for large areas but it is more effective for smaller climbers, where a limited area is covered.

HOW TO USE NETTING

Rigid plastic netting is suitable for covering brick or stone walls as well as wooden walls and panel fences. It can also be wrapped around poles or pillars, to give plants something to grip. You can string netting between upright posts, as a temporary support for annual climbing plants such as sweet peas, but it is not really suitable for a permanent structure of this sort.

Netting is readily available from garden centres and nurseries. It can generally be bought in green, brown or white, which allows you to choose a colour that matches the wall, so that the netting does not show up too obviously. It is also possible to buy special clips, which make fixing the netting to a surface very simple.

The clips are designed to be used either with masonry nails or with screws. They have the advantage that they hold the netting away from the wall, so that there is room for the plant to climb through it or wrap its tendrils round the mesh, whereas if the netting is nailed directly to the wall there is no space between them.

A further advantage of this method of fixing is that the net can be unclipped and eased away from the wall, allowing the latter to be painted or treated

with preservative before the net is clipped back into position.

Plastic netting can be used either with plants that support themselves with tendrils or by twining, or with plants that need to be tied in. It does not look as attractive as the more expensive wooden trellising but, once it has been covered with the climber, it is not noticeable, especially if the right colour has been chosen. After a few years you will not be able to see the netting at all; it will be covered in a mass of foliage and flowers.

1 Position the first clip just below the top of where the net will be and drive in a masonry nail. Alternatively, drill a hole, plug it and screw the clip into it.

2 With a spirit level, mark the position of the other upper clip, so that it is level with the first. Fix the second clip.

3 Place the top of the net in position, with one horizontal strand in the jaw of the clip. Press it home so it is securely fastened. Repeat with the other clip.

4 Smooth the net down against the wall and mark where the next set of clips will come. They should be at about 60 cm (2 ft) intervals down the wall. Move the net out of the way, fix the clips and press the net into the clips. Follow the same procedure with the bottom clips.

5 When the netting is securely in place, train the climber up into it. Even those that are self-supporting may need tying in to get them going. If the plant is a little way out from the wall, train it towards the netting along canes.

Above: *Netting is rather ugly and it is best used with vigorous climbers that will soon cover it. Here, the netting has only been used well above the ground, where the main support is needed. Unsightly supports won't show around the base of the climbers, where the main stems make an attractive feature in their own right.*

Trellis and Fences

One of the simplest and yet most decorative ways of displaying climbers is to grow them over free-standing trellises or fences. Used in the garden, to define its major routes, this is an impressive way of bringing planting right in to the garden's fundamental structure.

BOUNDARIES AND SCREENS

Fences tend to be functional, in that they create a boundary; this is usually between the garden and the outside world but a fence is sometimes used as an internal divider. Many existing fences are ugly and covering them with climbers is a good way of hiding this fact. Those erected by the gardener need not be ugly but they still provide an opportunity for climbers.

Trellises are usually much more decorative than fences. They are not so solid and allow glimpses of what lies on the other side. They are either used as internal dividers within the garden, as screens, or simply as a means of supporting climbers. Used in this way, trellis can make a tremendous contribution to a garden design, as they can provide horizontal as well as vertical emphasis. As screens, they are useful for disguising eyesores such as fuel tanks, garages or utility areas.

ERECTING TRELLIS

The key to erecting a good trellis is to make certain that it is firmly planted in the ground. Once covered with climbers, it will come under enormous pressure from the wind and will work loose unless firmly embedded in concrete. Do not try to take a short cut by simply back-filling the post-hole with earth; unless the trellis is in a very protected position, it will eventually fall over. Panel fences are erected in a similar way.

Virtually any climber can be grown over trellis. But unless it is in a sheltered position, trellis will not offer the same protection as a wall to tender climbers.

1 Dig a hole at least 60 cm (2 ft) deep, deeper in light soils.

2 Put the post in the prepared hole and partly fill the hole with a dry-mix concrete. Check that the post is upright and not sloping, using a spirit level. Adjust the position of the post, if necessary, and then continue filling the hole, tamping down firmly as you go to hold the pole still.

3 Continue filling the hole with concrete, ramming it down firmly; frequently check that the post is still upright. The post should now be firm enough in the ground to work on and, once the concrete has "cured", it will be permanently secure.

4 Lay the panel on the ground, to work out where the next hole should be. Dig the hole, again to at least 60 cm (2 ft) deep.

5 Nail the panel on to the first post, while a helper supports the free end.

6 Place the second post in its hole and nail it to the panel, checking that the tops of the posts are level and the panel is horizontal. Fill the second hole with dry-mix concrete, tamping it down as you proceed. Check that the post is upright and adjust, if necessary.

7 Repeat the steps by digging the third post hole, nailing on the second panel, positioning and nailing the third post and so on, until the length of trellising is complete. This is more accurate than putting in all the posts and then fixing the panels, when, inevitably, some gaps will be too large and some too small.

Above: *Honeysuckles will quickly cover trellis.*

Hoops

Training over hoops allows you to direct the growth of the plant, so that it covers all the available space. If the plant is allowed to shoot heavenwards, the result can be disappointing, whereas, if you spread out the initial stems at the base when you first plant, you can encourage the plant to make a much better display.

THE AIMS OF TRAINING

Bending the new young growth into curving arches encourages flowering buds to be formed along the whole length of the stem, rather than just at the tip, as happens if the branch is tied in a vertical position. Frequently, new shoots will also develop from the curving stems and these should, in turn, also be tied into an arch, gradually encouraging the climber to cover the whole hoop. This will encourage a much thicker coverage and many more blooms.

Training plants over hoops helps keep their final height in proportion to the border in which they are growing. It is a very useful method for growing reasonably vigorous plants in a limited space. Very vigorous plants are best avoided; they will soon outgrow their space, however much training you do!

1 In early spring, make a series of hoops around the rose, pushing each end of the pole into the ground. The wood used should be pliable, hazel *(Corylus avellana)* being one of the best to use. Bend each stem carefully, so that it does not crack.

2 Allow each hoop to overlap the previous one.

3 Sort out the long shoots of the rose, carefully bend them over and then tie them to a convenient point on the hoop. In some cases, it may be easier to tie the shoot to a stem that has already been tied down.

4 To start with, the "bush" will look rather untidy but, gradually, the leaves will turn to face the light and it will produce new buds all along the upper edges of the curved stems.

5 Gradually the plant will fill out, and by midsummer it should be a mass of blooms. Every year, remove a few of the older stems and tie in all new ones. After a few years, remove the old hoops and replace them with new ones.

Above: *Roses grown over hoops form a dense bush that is covered with flowers. Here* R. *'Isphahan' puts on a good display of flowers as well as putting on plenty of new growth for the following year.*

Growing Climbers up Tripods

Tripods provide a useful opportunity for growing climbers in borders and other areas of limited space. A tripod helps to create vertical emphasis in gardens and may become a striking focal point if eye-catching climbers are allowed to cover it with foliage and flowers.

USING TRIPODS

Tripods can be formal, made to a classic design, or they can be made from rustic poles. The former are better where they are still partly on show after the climber is in full growth. The latter, on the other hand, in spite of their rustic and informal charm, are more suitable for carrying heavy, rampant climbers that will cover them completely. Tripods provide a more substantial support than a single pole.

More formal designs can be bought complete, ready to be installed in the garden. Tripods can, of course, also be made by the competent woodworker. A rustic-pole tripod is much more basic and can easily be constructed by most gardeners. They can be made to any height, to suit the eventual height of the plants and the visual aspects of the site.

Although any type of climber can be grown up a tripod, self-clingers would not be so good because there isn't enough flat surface for them to attach their modified roots. Tripods are ideal for carrying two or more climbers at once. If possible, choose climbers that flower at different times. Alternatively, choose two that flower at the same time but look particularly well together.

An ideal combination is a rose and a *Clematis viticella*. The latter is pruned almost to the ground each winter and so is still growing while the rose is in flower and, therefore, does not smother it. Later in the summer, the clematis comes into its own when the rose is past its best.

1 Position three posts in the ground. The distance apart will depend on the height; balance the two to get a good shape. The posts can be driven into the ground but a better job is done if you dig holes at least 60 cm (2 ft) deep. For a really solid job, backfill the holes with dry-mix concrete, but it will normally be sufficient just to ram the earth back around the poles.

2 Nail cross-pieces between the posts. These will not only help support the plants but also give the structure rigidity. Rails at 40–45 cm (15–18 in) apart should be sufficient for tying in stems. If you want more support for self-clingers, wrap a layer of wire netting around the structure. The plants will soon hide it.

3 When you nail the cross-pieces to the poles, the ends may well split if they have already been cut to the exact length. Nail the pieces on first and then cut them to the right length. Alternatively, cut to length and then drill holes in the appropriate places before nailing to the poles.

4 Plant the climbers in and around the tripod. Avoid planting them too close to the upright poles as the earth here will either be rammed down hard or have been replaced with concrete. Before planting, dig in some well-rotted organic material.

5 Water all the plants in well. If the weather continues dry, keep watering until the plants have become established. Always soak the ground well: a dribble on the surface will not help the plants send roots out into the surrounding soil.

6 The finished tripod will look a bit raw at first but it will soon weather and become covered in plants.

CLIMBERS SUITABLE FOR TRIPODS
Clematis
Humulus (hop)
Lonicera (honeysuckle)
Rosa (roses)
Solanum jasminoides
Tropaeolum (nasturtiums)
Vitis (vines)

Right: *As an alternative, a tripod can be constructed so that the tops meet, forming a three-sided pyramid. Here, Clematis 'Jackmanii' is seen clambering up such a design; once fully grown, the clematis will cover the support completely, so that the tripod cannot be seen.*

Simple Pillars for Climbers

A very effective way of displaying climbers is to grow them up a single pole, which is usually called a pillar. This can look very elegant and also means it is possible to grow a large number of climbers in a relatively small space. Pillars create vertical emphasis in borders or small gardens, without creating a barrier.

CLIMBERS FOR PILLARS

Clematis
Humulus (hop)
Lonicera (honeysuckle)
Rosa (roses)
Solanum jasminoides
Tropaeolum (nasturtiums)
Vitis (vines)

USING PILLARS

A surprising number of climbers are suited to growing up pillars. Most climbing roses, for example, look particularly good growing up them, although it is probably best to avoid vigorous climbers or rambling roses.

An advantage of using pillars for your climbers is that they are inexpensive and simple to erect and take down.

The pillar shown here is permanently positioned in a border but is possible to place the posts in a collar of concrete or a metal tube, so that they can be taken down during the winter when they are bare.

Movable columns are best suited to annuals or *Clematis viticella*, which can be cut down almost to the ground before the posts are removed. Permanent climbers, such as roses, will need a permanent structure.

If space is available, a very attractive walkway can be created by using a series of pillars along a path. This can be further improved by connecting the tops with rope, along which swags of climbers can grow. This is a very good way of growing roses and creates a very romantic, fragrant route through the garden. The effect is suited to formal designs, but is so soft and flowing that it gives a very relaxing feel.

1 Dig a hole at least 60 cm (2 ft) deep. Put in the post and check that it is upright. Backfill with earth, ramming it firmly down as it is filled. In exposed gardens, a more solid pillar can be created by filling the hole with concrete.

2 Plants can be tied directly to the post but a more natural support is created if wire netting is secured to the post. Plants such as clematis will then be able to climb by themselves with little attention from you other than tying in wayward stems.

3 Plant the climber a little way out from the pole, to avoid the compacted area. Lead the stems to the wire netting and tie them in, to get them started. Self-clingers will now take over but plants such as roses will need to be tied in as they climb. Twining plants, such as hops, can be grown up the pole without the wire.

Left: Clematis 'W.E. Gladstone' climbing up a pillar. If the pole was covered with wire netting the plant would have more to grip on, which would prevent it suddenly collapsing down the pole under its own weight as it may do later here.

Right: Although single-post pillars are rather slim, they can accommodate more than one climber. Here there are two roses, 'American Pillar' and 'Kew Rambler'. Another option is to choose one rose and a later-flowering clematis.

Above: Single-post pillars help to break up what would, otherwise, be a dull, rather two-dimensional border. Although it is only a thin structure, when clothed with a climber it becomes a well-filled-out, irregular shape, as this 'American Pillar' rose shows.

Growing Climbers Through Trees and Shrubs

In the wild, many climbing plants that are also used in the garden find support by scrambling up through trees and shrubs. In thick woodland or forests, they may grow to 50 m (150 ft) plus, in search of light. In the garden, supports of this height are rarely available, and, if they were, the flowers of the climbers using them would be out of sight.

CHOOSING GOOD PARTNERS

A smaller support is required for cultivated climbers in the garden, with a large apple tree, therefore, usually being the highest used. Clematis and roses will scramble through the branches, creating huge fountains of flowers. On a more modest scale, even dwarf shrubs can be used to support some low-growing climbers.

One of the advantages of growing climbers through shrubs is that it is possible to obtain two focuses of interest in one area. This is particularly true of early-flowering shrubs, which are relatively boring for the rest of the year. Through these, it is possible to train a later-flowering climber to enliven the area further on in the season. Clematis are particularly good for this, especially the later-flowering forms, such as the viticellas. These can be cut nearly to the ground during the winter, so that the shrub is relatively uncluttered with the climber when it is in flower itself earlier on in the next season.

Fruit trees that have finished their fruiting life can be given new appeal if you grow a rose through them. However, it is important to remember that old trees may be weak and that the extra burden of a large rose, especially in a high wind, may be too much for it to carry.

CLIMBERS SUITABLE FOR GROWING THROUGH TREES
Akebia
Clematis
Fallopia baldschuanica (Russian vine)
Humulus (hop)
Lonicera (honeysuckle)
Rosa (roses – vigorous varieties)
Solanum crispum
Solanum jasminoides

CLIMBERS SUITABLE FOR GROWING THROUGH SHRUBS
Clematis
Cobaea scandens (cathedral bells)
Eccremocarpus scaber (Chilean glory flower)
Ipomoea (morning glory)
Lathyrus odoratus (sweet peas)
Thunbergia alata (black-eyed Susan)
Tropaeolum (nasturtiums)
Vinca major

1 Any healthy shrub or tree can be chosen. It should preferably be one that flowers at a different time to the climber. Choose companions that will not swamp each other. Here, a relatively low *Salix helvetica* is to be planted with a small form of *Clematis alpina*. The two will make a delicate mix, especially the blue clematis flowers against the silver foliage of the *Salix helvetica*.

2 Dig the planting area at a point on the perimeter of the shrub and prepare the soil by adding well-rotted organic material. For clematis, choose a position on the shady side of the plant, so that its roots are in shade but the flowers will be up in the sun. Dig a hole bigger than the climber's rootball and plant it. Most climbers should be planted at the same depth as they were in their pots but clematis should be 5 cm (2 in) or so deeper.

3 Using a cane, train the clematis into the bush. Once the clematis has become established, you can remove the cane. Spread the shoots of the climber out so that it spreads evenly through the shrub, not just in one area.

4 If possible, put the climber outside the canopy of the shrub or tree, so that it receives rain. However, it is still important to water in the new plant and, should the weather be dry, to continue watering until the plant is established.

Above: *The beautiful white clematis 'Marie Boisselot' grows up through a small apple tree.*

Archways

Arches are very versatile features in a garden and are well suited for growing a variety of climbers. Archways can be incorporated into a dividing feature, such as a wall, hedge or fence, or can be free-standing along a path as nothing more than a means of supporting climbers.

USING ARCHES

Archways exert a magnetic effect on visitors to your garden. No matter how interesting the area you are in, an archway draws the eye to what lies beyond. It creates mystery with tantalizing glimpses of other things.

Those forming entrances are important features. They are often the first thing that a visitor is aware of on entering a garden. Arches frame the scene beyond and create atmosphere. A cottage garden, for example, looks particularly fine when seen through a rose arch, while a formal town garden may be better suited to a simple arch of foliage, such as ivy.

The possibilities of creating an arch are almost endless. They can be purchased in kit form, made to order or made by the gardener. They can be made from metal, wood, brick or stone work. Plastic ones are also available, but are neither very attractive nor long lasting. Wooden ones present the biggest range. They can be formal ones created from panels of trellis, or informal ones made from rustic poles. The choice is normally limited by cost and the appearance that is required – climbers themselves will generally climb over anything.

Always choose or make one that is big enough for people to walk through when it is fully clad with climbers – which may stick out as far as 60 cm (2 ft) or more from the supports. Make certain that the supports are well sunk into the ground, preferably concreted in. When covered with a voluminous climber, an arch may be under great pressure from the wind and a storm may push over a badly constructed one, destroying your display.

Virtually any climbers can be used with archways, although over-vigorous ones can become a nuisance – they seem to be constantly growing across the entrance itself. Other types of climbers to avoid, unless there is plenty of room, are thorned roses which may cause injury, or coarse-stemmed plants such as hops. These can be dangerous to the unwary. If you want a rose, use something like 'Zéphirine Drouhin', which is thornless.

CLIMBERS FOR ARCHWAYS

Akebia
Campsis radicans
Clematis
Phaseolus (climbing beans)
Humulus (hop)
Lonicera (honeysuckle)
Rosa (roses)
Vitis (vines)

Above: *A simple arch, constructed from rustic poles and covered with a variegated ivy. The simplicity of the foliage allows the eye to pass through to the garden beyond, without distraction.*

Above: *Wisteria makes a good covering for an arch because, once it has finished flowering, its foliage still retains a great deal of interest. It is accompanied here by* Vitis coignetiae, *whose foliage turns a magnificent purple colour in autumn. Together, these climbers provide interest from spring to autumn.*

Above: *A golden hop*, Humulus lupulus aureus, *and a honeysuckle*, Lonicera periclymenum, *combine to decorate this archway. Again, interest should be provided from spring to autumn.*

Above left: *This wonderfully romantic arch seems to come from the middle of nowhere. The roses and long grass create a soft image that provides nothing but delight.*

Left: *Roses make excellent subjects for archways. Repeat-flowering ones provide the longest interest; once-flowering roses can be combined with late-flowering clematis, to extend the season.*

Arbours

An arbour is a framework over which climbers are trained to create a shady outdoor room. It can be just big enough to take a chair or bench, but best of all is an arbour large enough to accommodate a table and several chairs, where you can sit and linger over alfresco meals.

CLIMBERS FOR ARBOURS

Clematis (some fragrant)
Fallopia baldschuanica (Russian vine – very vigorous)
Hedera (ivy – evergreen)
Humulus (hop – dies back in winter)
Lonicera (honeysuckle – many fragrant)
Rosa (roses – many fragrant)
Vitis (vines – some fruiting)

DESIGNING AN ARBOUR

The structure can be of metal or wood or the arbour can have brick or stone piers with a wooden roof. The design can be any shape that takes the fancy or fits the site. It may be triangular, semi-circular, rectangular or octagonal, to suggest but a few. The climbers can be any that you like. If you do not like bees, stick to climbers grown for their foliage. In areas designed for relaxation, fragrant climbers are most welcome. Honeysuckle provides a delicious scent, particularly in the evening. Jasmine is another good evening plant. For daytime enjoyment, fragrant roses are ideal.

An arbour may have to remain in place for many years, so make sure you build it well. Take trouble to use timbers treated with preservative (not creosote, which may kill many climbers) and make certain that it is a strong design, well supported in the ground. As with similar structures covered in heavy climbers, the wind can wreak havoc on weak construction.

Right: *Here, the overhanging fig,* Ficus carica, *and the surrounding rose, clematis and other climbers create an intimate area for sitting and relaxing, which fulfils all the functions of an arbour, even though there is no supporting structure.*

Above: *This arbour is dappled with shade from a number of roses. It is big enough for small supper parties as well as simply sitting in the evening with a drink.*

Above: *A large arbour, built for entertaining, this example is covered in a variety of climbers, including a purple grapevine. This provides a wonderfully dappled shade, as well as colourful foliage and grapes at the end of the autumn.* Clematis montana *supplies the colour in the spring and early summer.*

Above: *A dual-purpose arbour: the newly planted beans will provide shade during the hotter part of the year, as well as a constant supply of runner beans for the kitchen. As a bonus, the flowers provide an added attraction.*

Walkways and Pergolas

Extending the use of arches and trellis brings the possibility of pergolas and walkways. This is an ideal way of providing a shady path. On the whole, these are not suitable for the smaller garden, although it is surprising what can be achieved with a bit of imagination.

USING WALKWAYS AND PERGOLAS

Walkways are open pergolas, with no roof. They can be double-sided, that is, down both sides of a path, or you can use a single piece of trellis down one side. The simplest way is to build them out of either trellis or rustic poles. For a romantic version, use a series of pillars linked with swags of ropes.

Both can become massive structures that have to support a great deal of weight, especially when there is a strong wind blowing, so it is important to make certain that, whatever the material, the walkway or pergola is well constructed.

A wide range of climbing plants can be used to clothe the pergola or walkway; fragrant plants are especially pleasing. Roses are ideal, as long as they are either thornless or well tied in so that they do not catch passers-by with their thorns. Evergreen climbers, such as ivy, make a dark and intriguing tunnel and will keep passers-by dry in wet weather throughout the year.

Right: *An arch leads through into another part of the garden. The poles are covered with* Rosa *'American Pillar' and* R. *'Albertine'. On the side of the arch is* Clematis *'Alba Luxurians'.*

Above: *Clematis tumbling over the corner of a pergola. Here, C. 'Etoile Violette' combines with some late flowers of* C. montana *to create an attractive picture.*

Above: *Colourful foliage makes a long-lasting covering for a pergola. Here* Vitis vinifera *'Purpurea' creates an attractive screen up a wooden pillar. As the year proceeds, the colour of the foliage will deepen, so there is a change of appearance, even without flowers.*

Above: *A romantic walkway created from a series of arches, passing along a clipped path through long grass. The arches provide a delightful tunnel effect, while the statue at the end draws the eye and adds to the romantic image.*

Temporary Supports

It is not always desirable to have fixed screens or supports for climbers. It can be fun to move them around the garden, using a different position each year. This allows a much more flexible design. While this is not really practical with perennial climbers, especially those that might take several years to establish themselves, it is entirely possible with annuals.

USING TEMPORARY SUPPORTS

In some cases, temporary supports can undertake two functions at once: to provide an attractive screen and to provide vegetables for the kitchen. Thus, peas and beans make good traditional subjects, while more novel ideas might include climbing marrows, courgettes (zucchini), gourds (squashes) and cucumbers.

Temporary screens are easy to make and a variety of materials can be used. Many are rustic in nature, such as pea-sticks simply pushed into the ground or traditional bean poles tied together in a row or wigwam (tepee). More modern materials would include plastic netting held on poles or a metal frame. However, it is best not to use materials that are unattractive, as the plants trained up temporary supports do not often get under way until the early summer, not covering them until midsummer.

Temporary structures can also be used for a few perennials that are cut to the ground each year, such as the everlasting pea *Lathyrus latifolius* or some of the clematis that are either herbaceous or a pruned to near the ground each year. Since the latter can grow quite tall, they can be supported by large branches stuck in the ground, to imitate small trees.

Left: *Climbing plants can often be used in this somewhat more horizontal way than is usual. It is an ideal way to utilize space left after spring flowers have finished blooming.*

Above: *A typical bean row, with the scarlet-flowered runner beans climbing up poles that have been tied together for support. The poles can be kept for several seasons before they need to be replaced.*

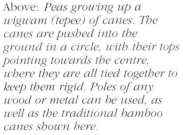

Above: *Peas growing up a wigwam (tepee) of canes. The canes are pushed into the ground in a circle, with their tops pointing towards the centre, where they are all tied together to keep them rigid. Poles of any wood or metal can be used, as well as the traditional bamboo canes shown here.*

Above right: *Sweet peas growing up a temporary screen of pea-sticks. Hazel (Corylus avellana) is one of the best types of wood, but any finely branched sticks will do. They usually only last one season and then need to be replaced.*

Right: *A framework of hazel sticks have been woven into a dome, over which a clematis is growing.*

Growing Climbers in Containers

Although most climbers are grown in the open ground, there is no reason why they should not be grown in containers. This is a particularly good idea for a balcony, roof garden or patio. While it is not really feasible to grow vigorous plants in this way, a surprising number of climbers are suitable.

SUPPORTING CLIMBERS IN POTS

The main problem when growing climbers in pots is finding a method of supporting the plant. If they are only short plants or annuals, such as black-eyed Susan (*Thunbergia*) or nasturtiums, it is perfectly feasible to include the support in the container. You can use canes or a V-shaped piece of trellising, burying the lower end in the pot.

For more vigorous plants, set the containers against a wall on which trellis has been fixed. An alternative is to have strings or tall canes rising from the pot to some suitable fixing on the wall.

One of the main secrets of success with container climbers is to keep them watered well. Feeding also becomes very important, as constant watering leaches out many of the nutrients in the soil.

1 To ensure that the compost in the container is adequately drained it is important to place a layer of small stones or broken pots in the bottom. This will allow any excess water to drain away quickly.

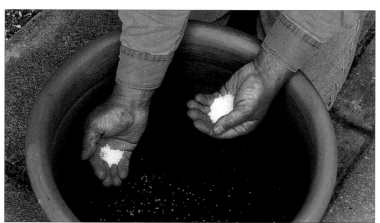

2 Partly fill the pot with a good-quality potting compost (soil mix). Add to this some water-retaining granules and stir these into the compost. Use the quantity recommended on the packet. The granules will expand when they become wet and hold the moisture until the plant wants it, without making the soil too wet, something that most plants hate.

3 Put the narrow end of the trellis into the container. The trellis will be held in position by the weight of the compost, so the base should be as low down in the pot as possible. This type of frame is not suitable for tall, narrow pots, which may be blown over easily.

4 Put the plant in position so that the top of the rootball comes level with the intended surface of the compost. Put in the remaining compost and lightly firm it down. Train the stems of the climber against the trellis and tie them in, if necessary.

5 Water the pot and top it up with compost (soil mix) if the level falls. Cover the top with pebbles or gravel, partly to give it a pleasant appearance but also to help suppress weeds and make watering easier. When creating such a display, put it in its final position before you fill the container as the complete container may be very heavy.

6 As an alternative, fix a piece of trellis to a wall and stand the pot next to it. This will take heavier climbers and be less inclined to blow or fall over. Being next to a wall may put the pot in a rain shadow, however, so be prepared to water it even if you have had rain.

Above: *Grouping containers together presents an attractive display. Here,* Clematis *'Prince Charles' is planted in a chimney pot next to some potted chives.*

Above: *A variety of different frameworks can be used in large containers, to support annual and temporary climbers. The metal frameworks will last the longest but will be most expensive. The willow wicker support, at the back of the group, is attractive in its own right.*

Plant List

Plant lists for specific types of climbers (e.g. fragrant climbers) are given in the relevant sections.

Where only the genus is given several species and cultivars are suitable.

ac = annual climber
c = climber
wf = wall fruit
ws = wall shrub

YELLOW-FLOWERED CLIMBERS AND WALL SHRUBS
Abutilon megapotamicum (ws)
Azara dentata (ws)
Billardiera longiflora (c)
Clematis (c)
  C. 'Moonlight'
  C. 'Paten's Yellow'
  C. rehderiana
  C. tangutica
  C. tibetana

Clematis tangutica

Eccremocarpus scaber (c)
Fremontodendron
  californicum (ws)
Humulus lupulus 'Aureus' (c)
Jasminum (c & ws)
Lathyrus (ac & c)
Lonicera (c)
Magnolia grandiflora (ws)
Piptanthus laburnifolius (ws)
Rosa (c)
  R. 'Dreaming Spires'
  R. 'Emily Grey'
  R. 'Gloire de Dijon'
  R. 'Golden Showers'
Thunbergia alata (ac)
Tropaeolum (ac)

Lonicera japonica *'Halliana'*

ORANGE-FLOWERED CLIMBERS AND WALL SHRUBS
Bignonia capreolata (c)
Bougainvillea spectabilis (c)
Campsis (c)
Eccremocarpus scaber (c)
Lonicera (c)
Rosa (c)
  R. 'Autumn Sunlight'
  R. 'Danse du Feu'
Tropaeolum (ac)

RED-FLOWERED CLIMBERS AND WALL SHRUBS
Akebia quinata (c)
Bougainvillea spectabilis (c)
Callistemon citrinus (ws)
Camellia (ws)
Chaenomeles (ws)

Clematis *'Madame Julia Correvon'*

Clematis (c)
  C. 'Niobe'
  C. 'Ruby Glow'
Clianthus puniceus (ws)
Crinodendron hookerianum (ws)
Desfontainea spinosa (ws)
Eccremocarpus scaber (c)
Erythrina crista-galli (ws)
Lathyrus (ac & c)
Lonicera (c)
Phaseolus coccineus (ac)
Rhodochiton atrosanguineum (c)
Ribes speciosum (ws)
Rosa (c)
  R. 'American Pillar'
  R. 'Danny Boy'
  R. 'Excelsa'
  R. 'Galway Bay'
  R. 'Symphathie'
Tropaeolum (ac & c)

Clematis *'Duchess of Albany'*

Clematis *'Comtesse de Bouchard'*

PINK-FLOWERED CLIMBERS AND WALL SHRUBS
Bougainvillea spectabilis (c)
Camellia (ws)
Chaenomeles (ws)
Cistus (ws)
Clematis (c)
  C. 'Comtesse de Bouchard'
  C. 'Hagley Hybrid'
  C. 'Margot Koster'

Lathyrus grandiflorus

Hoya carnosa (c)
Jasminum beesianum (c)
Jasminum x *stephanense* (c)
Lapageria rosea (c)
Lathyrus (ac & c)
Lonicera (c)
Malus (wf)
Mandevilla splendens (c)

Nerium oleander (ws)
Prunus (wf)
Rosa (c)
   R. 'Albertine'
   R. 'Bantry Bay'
   R. 'New Dawn'
   R. 'Pink Perpétue'
   R. 'Zéphirine Drouhin'

Vinca major

BLUE-FLOWERED CLIMBERS AND WALL SHRUBS
Aloysia triphylla (ws)
Ceanothus (ws)
Clematis (c)
   C. 'Beauty of Richmond'
   C. 'Lady Betty Balfour'
   C. macropetala
   C. 'Mrs Cholmondeley'
   C. 'Perle d'Azur'
Hydrangea aspera villosa (ws)
Ipomoea (ac)
Lathyrus (ac & c)
Passiflora caerulea (c)
Plumbago capensis (c)
Rosmarinus officinalis (ws)
Solanum crispum (ws)
Solanum jasminoides (c)
Sollya fusiformis (c)
Teucrium fruticans (ws)
Vinca major (c)
Wisteria (c)

PURPLE-FLOWERED CLIMBERS AND WALL SHRUBS
Clematis (c)
   C. 'Etoile Violette'

Clematis *'Lasurstern'* and Clematis *'Nelly Moser'*

   C. 'Gipsy Queen'
   C. 'The President'
Cobaea scandens (ac)
Lathyrus (ac & c)
Rosa (c)
   R. 'Bleu Magenta'
   R. 'Veilchenblau'
   R. 'Violette'
Solanum dulcamara 'Variegata' (c)

Vitis vinifera *'Purpurea'*

GREEN-FLOWERED CLIMBERS AND WALL SHRUBS
Garrya elliptica (ws)
Hedera (c)
Itea ilicifolia (ws)
Ribes laurifolium (ws)
Vitis (c)

Clematis *'Mrs George Jackman'*

WHITE-FLOWERED CLIMBERS AND WALL SHRUBS
Camellia (ws)
Carpenteria californica (ws)
Chaenomeles (ws)
Cistus (ws)
Clematis (c)
   C. 'Edith'
   C. 'Miss Bateman'
   C. 'Snow Queen'
Clianthus puniceus (ws)
Cotoneaster (ws)
Dregea sinensis (c)
Fallopia baldschuanica (c)
Hoheria (ws)
Hoya carnosa (c)
Hydrangea anomala petiolare (c)
Jasminum (c & ws)

Clematis florida *'Sieboldii'*

Lathyrus (ac & c)
Mandevilla suaveolens (c)
Myrtus (ws)
Nerium oleander (ws)
Pileostegia viburnoides (c)
Prunus (wf)
Pyracantha (ws)
Pyrus (wf)
Rosa (c)
   R. 'Albéric Barbier'
   R. 'Kiftsgate'
   R. 'Mme Alfred Carrière'
Solanum jasminoides 'Album' (c)
Trachelospermum (c)
Wisteria (c)

Rosa *'Iceberg'* and Clematis tangutica

Clematis *'Marie Boisselot'*

ACKNOWLEDGEMENTS

The publishers would like to thank the following for their permission to photograph their plants
and gardens: Hilary and Richard Bird; Mr & Mrs R Cunningham; Chris and Stuart Fagg; Merriments
Gardens; Christopher Lloyd; Eric Pierson; the RHS Garden, Wisley; Mavis and David Seeney and Lyn and Brian Smith.

They would also like to thank the following people for allowing their pictures (to which they own the copyright) to be reproduced in this book:
Peter McHoy for the pictures on pages 8, 9bl, 17r, 34, 35, 36tr & bl, 45b, 49bl, 52br, 54b, 55r, 56br, 57bl, 58tr & bl, 92c and 93tl;
Jonathan Buckley for the pictures on pages 32bl, 44l, 46bl, 48bl, 54tl, 56tl, 57tl, 60bl and 61r;
Richard Bird for the picture on page 41br.